MORAL ABSOLUTES

The Père Marquette
Lecture in Theology
1989

MORAL ABSOLUTES
Catholic Tradition, Current Trends, and the Truth

by

WILLIAM E. MAY

Ordinary Professor of Moral Theology
The Catholic University of America

MARQUETTE UNIVERSITY PRESS
MILWAUKEE, WISCONSIN

Dedicated to the memory of
Paul Ramsey,
a great Methodist theologian,
and
John R. Connery, S.J.,
a masterful Catholic theologian,
both staunch defenders of the
truth of moral absolutes

Library of Congress Catalogue Card Number: 88-64163

Copyright © 1989
Marquette University Press
Milwaukee, Wisconsin 53233

Manufactured in the United States of America

ISBN 0-87462-544-0

Foreword

The 1989 Père Marquette Lecture in Theology is the twentieth in a series commemorating the missions and explorations of Père Jacques Marquette, S.J. (1637-75). This series of annual lectures was begun in 1969 under the auspices of the Marquette University Department of Theology.

The lecture series is endowed by the Joseph A. Auchter Family Endowment Fund. Joseph Auchter (1894-1986), a native of Milwaukee, was a banking and paper industry executive and a long-time supporter of education. The fund was established by his children as a memorial to him.

The 1989 lecture was delivered at Marquette University on April 9, 1989, by Dr. William E. May, Ordinary Professor of Moral Theology at the Catholic University of America. Born in 1928, Professor May began his career as a philosophical and theological editor, working principally with the Bruce Publishing Company in Milwaukee. In 1968 he completed a doctorate in philosophy at Marquette University. He has taught at the Catholic University of America since 1971.

Professor May has written or co-authored more than a dozen books, including *Becoming Human: An Invitation to Christian Ethics* (1975); *Human Existence, Medicine, and Ethics* (1977); *Sex, Marriage, and Chastity* (1981); *Catholic Sexual Ethics* (1985); and *The Teaching of Humanae Vitae: A Defense* (1988). His many scholarly articles address such issues as the natural law, Thomas Aquinas's moral thought, contemporary fundamental moral theology, and marital, sexual, and medical ethics. The recipient of numerous academic awards and honors, including the 1980 Cardinal Wright Award from the Fellowship of Catholic Scholars and the 1983 Thomas Linacre Award from the National Federation of Catholic Physicians' Guilds, he is currently a member of the International Theological Commission and president of the Fellowship of Catholic Scholars.

In this lecture Professor May argues that there are absolute moral norms that unconditionally proscribe specific kinds of human action. After finding that the Catholic tradition from the early church through Vatican Council II has consistently affirmed the existence of moral absolutes, Professor May considers and evaluates the reasons many contemporary Catholic moral theologians give for denying that moral absolutes exist. He concludes that since none of these reasons is persuasive, and since we determine our moral identities through our free actions, we should recognize the existence of absolute moral norms permitting only those actions compatible with human good and proscribing any action that would make us evildoers.

RONALD J. FEENSTRA

Acknowledgments

I wish to acknowledge my gratitude to the faculty of the Department of Theology, Marquette University, for inviting me to give the Père Marquette Theology Lecture for 1989. Professor Ronald J. Feenstra of Marquette took great care in preparing my manuscript for the printer and made numerous suggestions to help the text flow more smoothly. Marquette's Professor Wanda Cizewski also made many helpful suggestions and corrections. I wish here also to thank particularly Germain Grisez and John Finnis, not only for their scholarly and enlightening writings on the subject of moral absolutes but also for their friendship, support, and help. I am also, of course, grateful to my wife, Patricia, and my children for their constant support and encouragement.

MORAL ABSOLUTES
Catholic Tradition, Current Trends, and the Truth

The expression "moral absolutes" desig-
nates moral norms that identify certain types
of action which are possible objects of choice
as always morally bad, and specify those types
of action without employing in their descrip-
tion any morally evaluative terms. Deliberately
killing the innocent, having intercourse with
someone other than one's spouse (i.e.,
adultery), making babies by *in vitro* fertiliza-
tion or by artificial insemination, and using
contraception are examples of types of action
specified by norms of this kind. Although
these norms, and others like them, are proposed as true by the magisterium of the
Church, their truth is denied by many contemporary moral theologians. These norms are
called "absolute" because they unconditionally
and definitively exclude specifiable kinds of
human action as morally justifiable objects of
choice. They are said to be true *semper et pro*
(or *ad*) *semper*. The types of action identified
by such norms are called "intrinsically evil

acts."[1] Although exceptions to these norms are logically possible, they are morally excluded. Thus, these norms are also called "exceptionless."

The central question is this: are there in truth norms of this kind? Many today say "no," whereas many others, including the magisterium, say "yes." In what follows I intend to do the following: (1) provide evidence that the Catholic tradition has consistently affirmed moral absolutes; (2) present the reasons advanced by many contemporary theologians (hereafter called "revisionist" theologians) to support their denial of such absolutes; (3) offer a critique of these reasons; and (4) show that moral absolutes are required by the basic principles of the moral life.

I. Moral Absolutes in the Catholic Tradition

To begin, I will briefly review relevant material on moral absolutes from the patristic and medieval periods, and from Suarez through the manualists whose moral thought shaped the modern Catholic tradition up to the time of Vatican Council II.

1. The Early Christian and Patristic Period

Early Christian tradition, beginning with the *Didache* in the second century and continuing through the Fathers, both East and West, definitely affirmed that there are moral absolutes. This can be seen by examining the teaching of early Christian writers and the Fathers on such specific issues as abortion, infanticide, adultery, fornication, and contraception. I propose to present evidence supporting this claim by examining representative texts on abortion and infanticide (instances of human action entailing the deliberate killing of the innocent), concluding my exposition with a somewhat more extensive account of the thought of St. Augustine, who so profoundly influenced subsequent Catholic tradition in the West.

Early Christian writers regarded human life as a great and glorious gift from God, something good and of incalculable value. They likewise knew that among the precepts of the Decalogue was the commandment, "Thou shalt not kill" (Ex 20.13; Dt 5.17), a commandment given even more specific content within the Old Testament by the command, "You must not put the innocent and the just to death" (Ex 22.7; Dn 13.53), and deepened in its moral significance by the teaching of Jesus (Mt 5.21-22 and par.). Of special moral horror was the deliberate killing of unborn and newborn human life (that is, abortion and infanticide). Many texts from early Christian tradition can be cited to show the moral outrage that these types of action provoked.[2] I will select just a few that illustrate the tradition regarding the absoluteness of the norms proscribing the deliberate killing of the innocent (and such sexual acts as fornication, sodomy, and adultery as well).

The first is a striking text from the *Didache*:

> You shall not kill. You shall not commit adultery. You shall not give yourself over to the corruption/destruction of boys, nor to fornication. . ., nor to making magic, nor to making "potions." You shall not kill the child by corruption/destruction, nor kill it at birth.[3]

The "corruption/destruction" of a child refers to abortion, since infanticide is specifically excluded immediately afterward. The making of magic and of potions refers to a variety of actions, probably including the use of steril-

izing and abortifacient drugs.[4] So in addition
to condemning in no uncertain terms peder-
asty and various forms of illicit sexual activity, this early Christian document has ex-
panded the explicit content of the Decalogue
to forbid actions ranging from sexual perver-
sions through the use of sterilizing and abortifacient drugs to killing a child before or after
birth.

Clement of Alexandria, after affirming
that "marriage is the desire to procreate
children, not the pointless spilling of sperm,"
stressed that Christians are to control their
desires and "refrain from destroying by vile
and vicious means the human progeny born
according to divine providence," adding that
"those women who take abortifacient drugs
to conceal their sexual perversity entirely lose
their humanity along with the fetus."[5]

Among Latin writers, Tertullian in his
Apology (a work dating from his Catholic
period) answers the charge that Christians
practice human sacrifice thus:

> For us, since homicide is forbidden, it is not even
> right to dissolve the conceptus in the womb while
> the blood is being formed into a man. It is an an-
> ticipation of homicide to prevent its being born, and

it makes no difference whether one takes away a
life already born or disturbs one in the process of
being born. He is also a man who is about to be one. [6]

Later, after the distinction between the
"formed" and the "unformed" fetus was made,
the suggestion arose that abortion prior to the
time the fetus was "formed" might not be evil.
This suggestion was promptly rejected. Thus,
in the East Basil had this to say: "The one
destroying a fetus by deliberate design is
judged guilty of murder. Whether it is formed
or not makes no difference to us."[7] Similarly,
John Chrysostom made no distinction in the
stages of unborn human life. He condemned
as something "even worse than murder" the
act that "does not take away life already born
but prevents its being born."[8]

The same was true in the West. Ambrose,
in his *Hexameron*, while speaking of birds,
draws a moral lesson for the faithful. After
noting how birds shelter and protect their
young, Ambrose contrasts their behavior with
that of humans, among whom women nurse
only for a short time and wealthy women omit
nursing altogether. He observes that at times
poor women expose and disown their children
by infanticide, and he then adds, "Also the

rich, to prevent dividing their estate among many heirs, kill the fetus in the womb and snuff it out in the genital chamber of the womb by parricidal mixtures. So life is taken away even before it is given."[9] In a commentary on the Gospel according to Luke, Ambrose insists that the effort to prevent the birth of conceived human life is a horrible affront to God, who is at work in the human womb when human life is conceived and developing: "He is at work – and you would violate by your lust the secret of that sacred womb? Either imitate brute animals or reject God."[10] According to Ambrose abortion violates both the rights of the child and the creative will of God.

Augustine frequently discusses abortion. An important passage appears in a text in which he affirms that marriage is itself good and that it uses sexual desire well for the procreation of children. He considers it a fault – but one that is "pardonable" or "venial" – for a married person to have intercourse merely to satisfy desire, provided that nothing is done by evil intent or action to prevent procreation. If married people try to prevent procreation, Augustine considers their action damnable, not pardonable or venial; and if a married couple never intended any other sort of life together he holds that they are in reality adulterers rather than spouses. In this context he notes how far some people go to prevent children:

> Having proceeded so far, they are betrayed into exposing their children, who were born against their will. They hate to nourish and retain those whom they were afraid they would beget. This infliction of cruelty upon their offspring, so reluctantly begotten, unmasks the sin which they had practiced in darkness, and drags it clearly into the light of day. The open cruelty reproves the concealed sin. Sometimes, indeed, this lustful cruelty, or cruel lust, resorts to such extravagant methods as to use poisonous drugs to secure barrenness, or else, if unsuccessful in this, to destroy the conceived seed by some means prior to birth, preferring that its offspring should rather perish than receive life, or if it was advancing to life within the womb, should be slain before it was born. [11]

Not only does Augustine absolutely condemn abortion and infanticide, [12] but he also explicitly rejects the claim that good intentions, anticipated good results, or a good purpose can justify doing deeds, like abortion and infanticide, that are wicked of themselves insofar as they require their perpetrators to set their wills against the good gifts of God's creation and against his plan for human existence. Thus it is always wrong to commit adultery, whether to gain mon[ey for the poor], to save an innocent person [from death, or] even to gain the secrets of he[retics with the] hope of vanquishing them a[nd of winning] their conversion.[13] Augustin[e argues that if] such things are licit then al[l ...] could become good if done for [... worthy ...] causes and reasons. Complete[ly rejecting this] view, Augustine says,

> Who would maintain that but o[ne ...] to subvert all human custom a[nd law? For, what] wicked deed, what disgraceful [...] pious sacrilege would not be decl[ared ...] and just? They would be done n[... im]punity but even with glory, and t[he actors of] them would not only not fear pun[ishment but would] even anticipate reward. Such wo[uld ... outcome] if once we grant that in all the ev[il ... men we] are not to ask *what* is done, bu[t merely *why* it is] done, so that whatever is found [to ... be] done for good reasons is not judged t[o be ...]

In many ways the though[t of Augustine,] as set forth in this passage f[rom his De] *Mendacium*, summarizes e[... early] tradition on moral absolutes [... No...] abortion and infanticide, as de[...]

of the innocent, horrible crimes and the norms proscribing them absolute, but also many other sorts of human actions – among them fornication, adultery, and contraception – are utterly opposed to God's loving plan for human existence and incompatible with the Christian way of life.

2. The High Middle Ages

Some revisionist theologians, among them Franz Scholz and John Dedek,[15] maintain that the great theologians of the Middle Ages, including Albert the Great, Bonaventure, and Thomas Aquinas, did not affirm the truth of moral absolutes or exceptionless moral norms. According to these modern commentators, the norms proposed by the great medieval theologians as absolute were merely "formal" norms, specifying the excluded acts by morally evaluative terms (e.g., "unjust killing") or by reference to vices or to passions contrary to right reason. In Dedek's opinion, the "full and coherent" affirmation of non-formal absolute norms in the medieval tradition can only be dated to the time of Durand of St. Pourcain (ca. 1325).[16]

The appeal by some revisionist theologians to the teaching of the great scholastics, and in particular that of St. Thomas, to support their denial of exceptionless norms will be discussed below, in an examination and criticism of the views of revisionist theologians. Here it must be said immediately that this claim simply does not square with the facts.

To show that this is so it suffices to note the reaction of the great medieval theologians to the opinion of an ancient commentator on Aristotle's *Nicomachean Ethics*, known to us only as the "Old Scholiast," who flourished around the beginning of the third century. The Old Scholiast had suggested in his commentary on Aristotle that it would be morally right to lie or even to have intercourse with a tyrant's wife in order to overthrow the tyrant and free his subjects. His views were brought to the attention of medieval theologians by Robert Grosseteste, thirteenth-century Bishop of Lincoln and classical scholar par excellence. When he came to translate the Scholiast's comment, he interjected the following strenuous objection:

> The Christian religion declares and holds that sin
> must not be committed, whether for the sake of pur-
> suing good (*utilitas*) or of avoiding loss. And so,
> since it is sin to lie and sin to have intercourse with
> another's wife (*alienae uxori misceri*), neither is in
> any way to be done. And so the teaching above is
> not teaching but error, in the example it proposes.
> For the evils of sin are not to be done for the sake
> of goods. [17]

Albert the Great, faced with the view of the
Old Scholiast, got right to the point: "What
the Commentator says is false." [18]

When Albert's pupil Thomas confronted
the view of the Old Scholiast in one of his
most mature works, *De Malo*, he shows quite
clearly that he does not consider "adultery,"
"fornication," "lying," or "murder" wrong
simply because such actions are *defined* as bad
(i.e., bad because they entail intercourse with
the "wrong" person or "unjustified" lying or
killing) but rather because such actions are
intrinsically evil. In an objection to his own
position he sets forth the following argument:

> Whatever is intrinsically sinful may not be done for
> any purpose however good – as Paul says in Romans
> 3.8. . . .But, as the Commentator on the Ethics says,
> a morally good man commits adultery with the
> tyrant's wife, so that the tyrant may be killed and
> the country liberated. Therefore, adultery is not

intrinsically wrong, still less any other act of
fornication. [19]

To this Thomas replies very simply: "The
Commentator is not to be followed in this
matter; for one may not commit adultery for
any good."[20]

I will say more about St. Thomas's position on moral absolutes below, where I
criticize appeals to his thought on the part of
revisionist theologians. Aquinas definitely (as
will be shown below) held that all the precepts
of the Decalogue are moral absolutes – so
much so that not even God can grant dispensations from them. That this was indeed the
view of St. Thomas is confirmed by Duns
Scotus (1266-1308), who taught that God can
grant dispensations from the precepts of the
second table of the Decalogue and clearly
thought that his view was opposed to
Aquinas's. Here I wish to say something about
Scotus's position on moral absolutes.

The Subtle Doctor clearly taught that, in
a very real and meaningful sense, there are
moral absolutes. He insisted that "all who are
subject to the divine law act inordinately if
they do not act in accord with it."[21] The
Decalogue, with its precepts not to kill, to

commit adultery, to steal, to bear false
witness, and so forth, pertains to the divine
law. According to Scotus these precepts must
be observed in every age of human history,
even by those who have not been given
knowledge of them by divine revelation: "All
were bound to these precepts, which were
written interiorly in the heart of each person,
or perchance were made known by some external teaching handed on from fathers to
children, even when they were not written in
any book."[22]

Nonetheless, Scotus, unlike Aquinas, held
that in another sense such moral precepts are
not absolute insofar as *God*, and God alone,
can grant true dispensations from them.[23]
God can do so, Scotus thought, because only
the first practical precepts of the natural law,
self-evidently known, and those conclusions
"necessarily following from them. . .can be
said to pertain to the natural law in the most
precise sense. . .and in these there can be no
dispensation."[24] But the very first practical
principle for Scotus is that God is to be loved
above all.[25] That God is to be loved above all
is a necessary truth that even God's will must
command.[26] Whatever follows by logical

necessity from this truth belongs absolutely
to natural law and is indispensable. Consequently, for Scotus, "no act is good of its kind
from its object alone save to love God. . .and
only that act is bad of its kind which is opposed to this act, with respect to the same
object, namely to hate God, which in no way
can be so circumstanced that it be good."
Accordingly, also, "every other act is [morally]
indifferent which concerns any other object,
and can be made good or bad by its circumstances."[27] Thus all actions proscribed by
precepts of the Decalogue pertaining to our
neighbor can be so "circumstanced" that they
can become morally good actions; and they
are so "circumstanced" when they are commanded directly by God.

By his *potentia ordinata*, according to
Scotus, God has in fact willed that men absolutely refrain from killing the innocent,
committing adultery, and so forth. Thus these
precepts of the Decalogue, while not pertaining by logical necessity to the natural law, are
valde consonans with it, and as a matter of
fact all men are strictly obligated to act in ac-
cordance with them. But by his *potentia
absoluta* God can will whatever does not con-

tain within itself a contradiction, that is, does not contradict the basic practical truth that God is to be loved above all things. Thus *God* can command that people kill the innocent, commit adultery, and so forth, and do so uprightly. But only God can so command, and only those to whom God directly reveals his will to dispense from the precepts that he has established by his *potentia ordinata* can justly choose to do such deeds. Scotus thought that this had in fact occurred when God ordered Abraham to sacrifice his son Isaac and instructed the Israelites to take the goods of the Egyptians.[28]

From this account of his thought, it should be clear that Scotus did in fact affirm the existence of moral absolutes, for he insisted that all men are strictly obligated to observe all the precepts of the Decalogue, including those proscribing the killing of the innocent, adultery, and bearing false witness against one's neighbor.

3. From Trent to the Eve of Vatican II

Francis Suarez (1548-1617), whose theory of natural law is profoundly different from that of St. Thomas, nonetheless strongly affirmed the existence of moral absolutes. According to him, natural law in its most precise sense is a judgment or set of judgments about what is or what is not in conformity with human nature and therefore to be done or avoided.[29] Such judgments are not merely indicative but truly preceptive or obligatory because "God, as the author of this nature, prescribes that that be done or avoided which reason declares to be done or avoided" and because "whatever is done contrary to right reason displeases God and the opposite [i.e., whatever is done in accord with right reason] is pleasing to him. Since the will of God is supremely just, that which is base cannot fail to be displeasing to him, whereas whatever is noble cannot fail to be pleasing to him."[30]

Moreover, Suarez held that certain actions are evil in themselves and can be known to be such by reason of their objects. As he put it, "In a human act there is some goodness or wickedness from the object precisely as such, insofar as it is consonant with or dissonant from right reason and by it can be so denominated."[31] Moreover, God "cannot not prohibit by some law those things that are intrinsically evil" because, "presupposing his

will to create a rational nature with
knowledge sufficient to doing good and evil
. . .God could not have not willed to proscribe
for such a creature acts intrinsically wicked
or not to prescribe acts necessarily good."[32]
In short, the intrinsic goodness or badness of
human acts consists in their conformity with
or disconformity from human nature. So long
as human nature exists, actions in conformity with it will be judged good and those not
in conformity with it will be judged bad. Since
God is the author of this nature, it necessarily
follows that whatever is judged in conformity
with it will be pleasing to him, and whatever
is judged contrary to it will be displeasing.
The precepts of the Decalogue embody judgments about some actions not in conformity
with human nature (e.g., adultery, killing the
innocent, theft) and other actions in conformity with it (e.g., honoring one's parents).
Such precepts are absolutely indispensable,
even by God.[33] Such precepts are moral
absolutes.

The line of thought developed by Suarez
is continued by moral theologians subsequent
to him up to the middle of the twentieth century. There is no need here to provide details

of this story, since it is acknowledged even by revisionist theologians. Germain Grisez and John C. Ford have amply demonstrated that the moral theologians represented in the manualist tradition clearly taught that there are moral absolutes, including that proscribing contraception.[34] Moreover, John T. Noonan's *Contraception: A History of Its Treatment by Catholic Theologians and Canonists* clearly demonstrates that from the beginning of the Christian era Catholic theologians held as absolute the norms proscribing adultery (understood as intercourse with someone who is not one's spouse), fornication, homosexual activity, and contraception.[35]

The Catholic tradition, as shown here, unambiguously affirmed that there are moral absolutes.

II. Current Debates: The Revisionist Position

Many contemporary Catholic theologians, among them some of the best known, deny that there are moral absolutes in the sense understood here. The reasons they give for this conclusion will be presented shortly.

First, however, I wish to note that all Catholic
moral theologians, until the middle 1960s, affirmed the existence of moral absolutes. Even
the authors of the so-called "majority report"
of the Papal Commission for the Study of
Population, the Family, and Natality, whose
views were made public in 1967, held to such
absolutes, for they clearly rejected as completely immoral the choice to engage in such
acts as anal or oral sex and nonmarital intercourse even though they argued that contraception could be a morally good choice for
married couples under certain conditions.[36]
Yet, as Charles E. Curran has correctly
noted,[37] the moral reasoning that they
employed to justify contraception by married
couples has led to the justification of other
kinds of choices that had previously, in the
Catholic tradition, been judged to be immoral
and contrary to absolute moral norms. Consequently, before examining more fully the
views of revisionist theologians, it seems to
me important to note some of the key claims
made by the authors of the celebrated
"majority report" of this papal commission.

    In one of their documents the authors had
this to say:

> To take his or another's life is a sin not because life
> is under the exclusive dominion of God, but because
> it is contrary to right reason *unless there is ques-*
> *tion of a good of a higher order*. It is licit to sacrifice
> a life for the good of the community. It is licit to
> take a life in capital punishment for the sake of the
> community. [38]

I call attention to this passage because the
principle set forth in it, namely, that one can
rightly destroy human life (or other human
goods) provided that one does so for the sake
of a greater good, looms large in the position
developed by revisionist theologians. I call
this the "Caiaphas" principle, although today
it is more commonly referred to as the
"preference principle" or the "principle of proportionate good."

The authors of the "majority report" also
argued that married couples may rightly con-
tracept individual conjugal acts so long as
their contracepted marital acts are ordered
to the expression of marital love, a love
culminating in fertility responsibly accepted.
Thus they say,

> When man intervenes in the procreative purpose of
> individual acts by contracepting, he does this with
> the intention of regulating and not excluding fer-
> tility. Then he unites the material finality toward

fecundity which exists in intercourse with the formal finality of the person and renders the entire process human. . . .Conjugal acts which by intention are
infertile[39] or which are rendered infertile [by use of
artificial contraceptives] are ordered to the expression of the union of love; that love, moreover,
reaches its culmination in fertility responsibly accepted. For that reason other acts of union are in
a sense incomplete and receive their full moral
quality with ordination toward the fertile act. . . .
Infertile conjugal acts constitute a totality with
fertile acts and have a single moral specification,
namely, the fostering of love responsibly toward
generous fecundity.[40]

This passage presents an understanding of
the "totality" of human acts that is, as we shall
see, quite central to the revisionist theologians' denial of moral absolutes. According to
the argument given here, there is a "material
privation" (or what later will be termed an
"ontic," "premoral," or "nonmoral" evil) in
contraceptive activity. However, the contraceptive intervention is only a partial aspect
of a whole series of contracepted conjugal
acts, and this entire ensemble "receives its
moral specification from the other finality,
which is good in itself [namely, the marital
union] and from the fertility of the whole conjugal life."[41] Put another way, this argument

claims that married couples who use contraception are not choosing to exclude
children selfishly from the marriage (or expressing what the authors elsewhere call pe-
joratively a "contraceptive mentality"). [42]
Rather, *what* they are doing – the moral
"object" of their act – is to "foster love responsibly toward a generous fecundity." And this
is something good, not bad.

This argument from the "majority report"
foreshadows one criticism made by revisionist
theologians of the traditional affirmation of
moral absolutes. Many revisionists claim that
the specific moral absolutes affirmed in the
tradition we have reviewed abstract *some*
elements from the total reality of a human
action. Reason, objectivity, and truth require
that an action be evaluated as right or wrong
only as a *totality* which includes all the circumstances and motivations, considered in
relation to *all* the "premoral" (but morally
relevant) goods and bads involved in that
totality, with a view to identifying the
behavior that will further human self-
realization and self-development [43] or at least
will not contradict or negate its own good purpose. [44] It likewise foreshadows their under-

standing of human action as a whole (comprised of various partial elements) that is given *moral* specification by its end or *telos*.

It is now appropriate to examine the moral vision of revisionist theologians and to see why they are led to deny the existence of moral absolutes as understood here.

These theologians, among them Böckle, Curran, Fuchs, Häring, Janssens, McCormick, Scholz, and Schüller, recognize some moral absolutes. They admit, first of all, absolutes in the sense of "transcendent" principles such as, "One must always act in conformity with love of God and neighbor," and "One must always act in accord with right reason."[45] They likewise acknowledge as absolute those "formal" norms that affirm what our inner dispositions and attitudes ought to be. It is thus always true that we should act justly, bravely, chastely, and so forth.[46] Such "formal" norms express the qualities that ought to characterize the morally upright person. They are concerned not with human acts but rather with the human person as a moral *being*.[47] In a sense they are, as Josef Fuchs has said, "exhortations rather than norms in the strict sense;"[48] and, as

Louis Janssens has noted, they "constitute the absolute element in morals."[49] These theologians also admit that there are absolute norms in the sense that some norms describe in morally evaluative language actions that morally good persons ought never to do. Thus, we ought never to *murder*, since murder is killing that is *unjust*. Likewise we ought never to have sexual intercourse with the *wrong* person or *selfishly* exclude children from marriage. Yet these norms are tautological and do not help us determine which specific kinds of killing are unjust, what specific kinds of intercourse are with the wrong person, what specific ways of behaving amount to a selfish exclusion of children from marriage. As Fuchs notes, these "absolute" norms are "parenetic," not instructive, and simply serve to remind us of what we already know and exhort us to avoid morally wrong actions and engage in morally right ones.[50]

What revisionist theologians deny is the truth of moral absolutes as norms that universally proscribe specifiable sorts of human action described in morally neutral language. They refer to these as "material" or "behavioral/material" norms. According to them such norms identify "physical acts" or "material acts" or "behavior" (including, in some cases, the "direct" or immediate effects thereof) described independently of *any* of the acting subject's purposes.[51] I shall return to this way of describing the "exceptionless" norms currently in dispute.

Why do revisionist theologians deny the truth of moral absolutes of this kind? The central reasons requiring this denial, each of which will be examined more fully, are these: (1) the historicity of human existence; (2) the logical implications of the basic moral norm or "preference" principle; (3) the "wholeness" or "totality" of a human act; and (4) the basic thrust of the best thinking in the Catholic tradition.

1. The Historicity of Human Existence

A basic question raised by revisionist theologians concerns the origin of "material" norms. How do we come to formulate such norms to begin with? How, in other words, do we come to the judgment that it is wrong to kill innocent persons or that it is wrong to have intercourse with someone who is not one's spouse? According to revisionist theologians norms of this kind are known inductively by the collaborative exercise of human intelligence by persons living together in communities and reflecting on shared human experiences.[52] Since material norms are discovered in this way, it follows that they are affected by human historicity and the open-ended, on-going character of human experience. There is indeed a "transcendent" aspect to human nature, insofar as the human person is called to "a steadily advancing humanization."[53] Nonetheless, "concrete" human nature, by reason of its historicity, is subject to far-reaching changes. It thus follows that no specific material norm, formulated under specific historical conditions, can be true and applicable universally and unchangeably.

From this, however, it does not follow that these norms are merely subjective and relative. Their objective truth corresponds to the actions they proscribe or prescribe as related to the "whole concrete reality of man" and of the particular, historical society in which people live.[54] Nevertheless, while these norms are true and objective, they cannot be absolute in the sense of being universally true

propositions about what human persons ought
or ought not to do in every conceivable condition. In fact, as Fuchs has said, "a strict
behavioral norm, stated as a universal, con-
tains unexpressed conditions and qualifica-
tions which as such limit its universality."[55]
Since human experience, reflection upon
which leads to the formulation of material
norms, is itself an ongoing, open-ended process, it follows, as another revisionist theologian says, that

> we can never exclude the possibility that future ex-
> perience, hitherto unimagined, might put a moral
> problem into a new frame of reference which would
> call for a revision of a norm that, when formulated,
> could not have taken such new experience into
> account.[56]

As a result, these norms are "valid only for
the most part."[57] Some describe actions that
for all practical purposes ought never to be
freely chosen – for instance, raping a retarded
child[58] or dropping nuclear bombs on centers
of civilian population[59] – and can be regarded
as "practical absolutes" or as "virtually exceptionless."[60] Nonetheless, because of the
historicity of human existence and the on-
going character of human experience, all

material norms must be regarded as open in principle to exceptions in the light of new historical conditions and new human experience.

2. The Basic Principle of Morality

Although they are not absolute, material moral norms are meant to guide us in our choices. They are intended to help us distinguish right from wrong and to understand how human actions bear upon human goods and values. Thus, in formulating such norms it is necessary to take into account how these human goods and values will be affected by possible courses of action. Revisionist theologians maintain that these human goods and evils (values and disvalues) are not, of themselves, moral in nature, although they are morally relevant. They constitute what these theologians call "premoral," "nonmoral," or "ontic" goods and evils, as distinct from moral good and evil, which consists essentially in the goodness or wickedness of the person as a moral being.[61] Thus goods such as human life itself, health, knowledge of the truth, beauty, and friendship are "nonmoral" goods and their deprivations are "nonmoral" evils.

The critical question is how we should determine, in developing material norms and in
judging which acts are legitimately exceptions
to them, which acts are morally right and
which are morally wrong, that is, which acts
promote and enhance these nonmoral goods
and values and which do not. There is need,
in other words, for a basic normative criterion
or fundamental moral norm to enable us to
distinguish morally acceptable alternatives
from those that are not. But what is this
criterion, and what implications does it have
with respect to the absoluteness of "material"
norms?

Recall now the principle evoked by the
authors of the "majority report" of the Papal
Commission for the Study of Population, the
Family, and Natality, namely, that it is
against right reason to take the life of an innocent person (a nonmoral good) or other
goods, "unless there is question of a good of
a higher order."[62] As formulated by revisionist theologians the principle operative in
this document has come to be known as the
"preference principle" or the "principle of proportionate reason." Bruno Schüller expresses
the matter in this way:

> Any ethical norm whatsoever regarding our deal-
> ings and omissions in relation to other men. . .can
> be only a particular application of that more univer-
> sal norm, "The greater good is to be preferred."[63]

According to this principle it is morally right
to intend a nonmoral evil, such as the death
of an innocent person, if this is required by
a "proportionately related greater good."
Thus, as Richard A. McCormick says,

> Where a higher good is at stake and the only means
> to protect it is to choose to do a nonmoral evil, then
> the will remains properly disposed to the values con-
> stitutive of human good. . . .This is to say that the
> intentionality is good even when the person, reluc-
> tantly and regretfully to be sure, intends the non-
> moral evil if a truly proportionate reason [i.e., good]
> for such a choice is present.[64]

This principle does not, revisionist theologians
claim, mean that a good end can justify morally evil means. But they hold that the intention and realization of a (nonmoral) good can
justify the doing of any nonmoral evil.[65]

It thus follows that every material norm
is subject to an exception clause: It is wrong
to kill an innocent person, to lie, to have sexual relations with a person not one's spouse,
and so forth *except* when doing so is required
in order to achieve a proportionately greater

good. Thus, some acts of direct abortion, mercy killing, and contraception can be morally right acts, provided they are done for the sake of a proportionate good.[66]

It is important to note that according to this basic norm it is morally right deliberately to intend a "nonmoral" evil for the sake of a proportionately greater "nonmoral" good. Although some revisionists, among them Peter Knauer[67] and Josef Fuchs,[68] claim that when one chooses to cause evil only as a means to a greater good and the evil is proportionate to the good, the evil or harm is *not intended*, most revisionists clearly admit that this principle justifies the deliberate intention to do nonmoral evil. One of these theologians, Richard A. McCormick, in the 1973 Père Marquette Theology Lecture, acknowledged that there is a significant difference between a will that intends evil and one that merely permits it. At that time he said,

> The will relates differently to what it intends and what it permits. . .the intending will (hence the person) is more closely associated with the evil than is a permitting will. This bespeaks (in some admittedly obscure way) a greater willingness that it [the evil] occur.[69]

As a result, he held at that time that a "greater" proportionate good is required if one is to intend the nonmoral evil than if one only "permits" or "indirectly intends" the non-moral evil associated with one's action.

McCormick sent his lecture to Bruno Schüller, who replied, "The person who is prepared to realize the good even by intend-ing evil is more willing that the evil exists, but only because he is more willing that the good exist."[70] Schüller likewise observed that "if someone is ready to bring the good into existence only by permitting the evil, it has been suggested [by McCormick] that he is less willing that the evil exist. Yet it must also be said that he is less willing that the good exist."[71] From all this Schüller concluded, "Therefore, I am strongly inclined to believe that in point of fact *'intend as a means' and 'permit,' when referring to a non-moral evil, denote exactly the same mental attitude.*"[72] In other words, according to Schüller there is *no* significant moral difference between an intending will and a permitting will.

Schüller's remarks so impressed McCor-mick that by 1978 he had abandoned his earlier view that an intending will more close-

ly relates the person to evil than does a permitting will, declaring that Schüller's objection to his original position was "fatal."[73] The
point Schüller seeks to make – one now shared
by McCormick – is this: since there is no
significant moral difference between
deliberately intending a "nonmoral" evil and
merely permitting it, the person who intends
and does evil for the sake of a proportionately
greater good has a greater love for the good
than one who refuses to intend and do evil
yet does at times permit it. And in their judgment this is an admirable trait of moral
character.

From all this it follows that the basic moral
principle of the revisionists logically leads to
the denial of moral absolutes. The refusal to
intend and do the ("nonmoral") evil these
absolutes proscribe would, in the judgment of
the revisionists, be a moral weakness when
intending and doing such evil is demanded by
the "preference principle."

3. The "Wholeness" or "Totality" of a Human Act

While the third consideration is closely
linked to the second, it is more fully developed

by some revisionists. This consideration is again foreshadowed in the "majority report" of the Papal Commission for the Study of Population, the Family, and Natality. Recall that in that report the majority had argued that a moral judgment about contraception could only be made in terms of the purposes of contracepted marital acts and the whole of the married life. The claim was made that if a couple deliberately prevents conception in individual conjugal acts in order to express marital union and orders these acts responsibly toward generous fecundity, one could properly say that *what* the couple was doing – the "object" of their moral choice – was "fostering love responsibly toward generous fecundity," even though this entailed the "material privation" (i.e., nonmoral evil) of individual acts of marital union of their openness to human life.[74]

Josef Fuchs, it should be noted, was one of the authors of this report. In his later articulation of revisionist thought, Fuchs insisted that the intending and doing of "premoral" evil cannot be morally evaluated in itself, because "an action cannot be judged morally in its materiality (killing, wounding,

going to the moon) without reference to the
intention of the agent; without this, we are
not dealing with a human action, and only of
a human action may one say in a true sense
whether it is morally good or bad."[75]

Here it is useful to recall that Fuchs and
other revisionists identify the controverted
moral absolutes that they deny with
"material" or "concrete behavioral" norms
specifying "physical acts" or "material acts,"
including, in some cases, their "direct" effects,
described independently of *any* purpose of the
agent.[76] In their judgment the tradition affirming such absolutes arbitrarily abstracted
some elements of an act from its total, concrete reality.[77] In addition, they claim that
this tradition falsely absolutized the human
goods protected by these alleged moral absolutes. Yet these goods, they say, while fundamental, are nonmoral, conditioned, created,
limited, and, in short, not absolute. According
to them the only absolute is to realize the good
which, in the concrete totality of the action,
is proportionately greater, that is, promises
the overall best proportion of nonmoral good
over nonmoral evil. Thus norms protecting
particular goods can never be more than

generalizations about what usually serves to promote human well-being; such norms have only a *prima facie* validity and may rightly be set aside if one correctly assesses the whole or totality of the action in question.[78]

Therefore, according to revisionists, if one properly evaluates the whole act and not merely partial aspects of it, one will see, for instance, that contraceptive intercourse, if done by married persons for a truly proportionate good, is only a partial aspect of a whole human act that can rightly be described as "fostering love responsibly toward a generous fecundity." Likewise, if a married couple resorts to contraceptive sterilization because any further pregnancy might endanger the mother's life, the choice to sterilize, when seen within the totality of what the couple is doing, can be described as a "marriage-stabilizing" act.[79] Accordingly, in the judgment of the revisionists, to absolutize norms proscribing contraception and contraceptive sterilization is simply to be blind to the wholeness of the concrete human act that is chosen and done. And the same is true of the other alleged moral absolutes, such as those proscribing the deliberate killing of the

innocent and having intercourse with someone who is not one's spouse. Such material
norms, while useful generalizations and valid
for the most part, ought to be set aside when
the action as a concrete whole demands that
this be done if the greater good is to be
served.

4. The "Best" in the Catholic Tradition

Revisionists willingly admit that the contemporary magisterium and the moral
theological tradition from the time of Durand
of St. Pourcain (ca. 1325) affirm the truth of
moral absolutes. [80] Yet they claim that such
absolutes were foreign to the mind of the
great Schoolmen, particularly St. Thomas
Aquinas, and that Vatican Council II likewise
advanced a moral stance favorable to the
denial of moral absolutes.

According to revisionists, St. Thomas
taught that specific moral norms are derived
from the truly universal principles they accept: "Good is to be done and pursued and evil
is to be avoided;" "One ought always act in
accord with right reason;" and "One must love
God and neighbor." But, they point out,
Thomas clearly taught that derived norms,

since they involve contingent particulars, are
true only for the most part,[81] that is, they are
useful generalizations but not universally true
moral norms.[82] In addition, they maintain
that since Aquinas considered the end to be
the formal element specifying the moral
goodness or badness of a human act, it follows
that for him an action really willed and done
coherently for the sake of a good end must
be morally good.[83] In fact, they say that
Aquinas, in justifying capital punishment and
killing in self-defense, recognized that it is,
at times, morally right to intend "ontic" or
"nonmoral" evil for the sake of a greater
"ontic" or "nonmoral" good.[84] Moreover, according to revisionists, Thomas understood
the precepts of the Decalogue, when considered as indispensable even by God, as
"formal" and not "material" norms, that is, as
norms identifying actions already morally
evaluated as "unjust" or "undue."[85] Finally,
Louis Janssens and Richard A. McCormick
point to a text from St. Thomas's *Quaestiones
Quodlibetales*[86] in which, they say, he explicitly recognizes that acts which, materially considered, involve the deformity of some nonmoral evil, can be made right by circum-

stances in which the nonmoral goods achieved will counterbalance the nonmoral evils involved.[87] It is thus clear, revisionists say, that St. Thomas, who represents the best in the Catholic tradition, denied the truth of moral absolutes as understood here.

Revisionists similarly hold that Vatican Council II supports their views. This Council, they say, recognized that the moral problems facing humankind are very complex, that their resolution can only be found by the collaborative effort of persons of good will, and that quite often the answers to them can only be tentative and inconclusive.[88]

For all these reasons – the historicity of human existence, the requirements of the basic moral norm or preference principle, the "wholeness" or "totality" of a human act, and the thrust of the "best" in the Catholic tradition – revisionist theologians deny the truth of moral absolutes. I turn now to a critical assessment of their views.

III. Critique of Revisionist Denial of Moral Absolutes

I intend to show that the arguments advanced by revisionist theologians to support their denial of moral absolutes are not cogent. I will take each one up in turn, but before doing so I want first to challenge their way of describing the moral absolutes whose truth is contested.

As we have seen, revisionists refer to these moral absolutes as "material" or "concrete behavioral" norms. According to them these norms identify "physical acts" or "material acts," including, in some instances, the "direct effects" of such acts, as physical events independent of *any* purpose of the agent. [89]

Both Catholic theologians who today defend the truth of moral absolutes and those who did so in the past, including St. Thomas (whose thought will be taken up more fully below), offer a much different account of these disputed norms, which they never call "material" or "behavioral" norms. According to these theologians, the human acts identified and morally excluded by such norms are not specified independently of the agent's will. Rather, they are specified "by the object" (*ex obiecto*), [90] and by "object" they mean exactly *what the agent chooses*, either as an end (*finis* or *finis remotus*) or as a means (*finis*

proximus).[91] The tradition affirming moral
absolutes held that such norms do not bear
upon acts "in their *natural* species" but rather
upon them "in their *moral* species (or
genus)."[92] The "form," the "intelligibility," of
such acts is not given by their nature as
physical events in abstraction from the
agent's understanding and willing, but from
their intelligibly chosen objects.[93] In this
tradition, moreover, "direct" does not mean
merely causal, material, or behavioral im-
mediacy but rather the adoption by the will
of what serves as either end or means.[94] For
example, the same *physical* or *material* act
(the "natural" species of the act), namely, sexual intercourse, can be, by reason of its
"object" (that is, by reason of the form or intelligibility it has as understood and willed by
the acting subject), either a marital act, an
act of incest, an act of adultery, or an act of
fornication.[95]

This matter will be clarified below. I call
attention to it here, at the beginning of my
critical assessment of revisionist thought, to
show the great difference between the way
traditional Catholic thought conceived of the
exceptionless norms or moral absolutes that

are the subject of this inquiry and the way revisionist theologians conceive of "material" norms.

1. Historicity and Moral Absolutes

A central claim of revisionist theologians is that the alleged moral absolutes or "material norms" are known inductively by the collaborative effort of persons living in communities in their reflection upon experience. Since such experience is open-ended, it follows, they claim, that "we can never exclude the possibility that future experience, hitherto unimagined, might put a moral problem into a new frame of reference which would call for a revision of a norm which, when formulated, could not have taken such experience into account."[96]

It is, of course, true that morality is to some extent relative to contingent social and historical reality. Thus societies, like individuals, make choices that both generate and limit moral responsibilities; new options become available as societies develop; better factual judgments often lead to new insight into moral responsibilities; and moral insight is often blocked by cultural biases and opened

by changed conditions.[97] But from this it does
not follow that all specific moral norms are
relative to contingent social and historical
reality. Revisionists themselves seek to avoid
a radical historical and cultural relativism by
appealing to the "transcendental" standard of
"a steadily advancing 'humanization' " or to
the self-realization of persons and of the communities in which they live.[98] But this vague
standard, as Germain Grisez has noted, lacks
the content "needed to determine what should
and what should not count as morally deter-
minative when one fills the formal concept of
human self-realization with the whole concrete reality of persons in society and their
world."

The argument that the open-ended character of experience precludes the possibility
of permanently true specific moral norms is
undoubtedly sound with reference to *some*
moral norms (not all moral norms, after all,
are absolute). This argument assumes that an
action can be morally evaluated only as a
totality (which includes all the circumstances
and ends considered in relationship to all the
nonmoral but morally relevant goods and
bads involved in that totality) for the purpose

of identifying the behavior that will foster human self-realization and self-development, [100] or that will not contradict or negate its own good purpose. [101] But this assumption, as will be shown below when I criticize the revisionist understanding of a human act as a "totality" or "whole," simply cannot stand up under scrutiny. Once an action has been properly identified, for instance, as an act of rape, one need not delay judgment about its morality until one knows why the rapist is choosing to do it, where it is done, in what century or millennium it occurs, and so forth. One can, on the basis of relevant moral principles, declare at once that it is simply an act a human person ought not freely choose to do.

Revisionists likewise claim that specific moral norms must be based on "concrete" human nature, which is subject to radical change, as opposed to "transcendent" human nature, and that consequently no specific moral norms based on concrete human nature can be universally and irreversibly true. [102] Those making this claim, however, do not explain clearly what "concrete," as opposed to "transcendent," human nature means. They

neither show how fundamental human goods
such as life itself, knowledge of the truth,
appreciation of beauty, friendship, and peace
might cease to be good for human persons,
nor explain how their claim about radical
change in human nature is compatible with
the unity of the human race or our solidarity
with Christ. They fail to show how this claim
can be reconciled with such basic truths of
Catholic faith as, for instance, that "all human
beings. . .have the same nature and the same
origin,"[103] a "common nature,"[104] and the
"same calling and destiny," and so, being fundamentally equal both in nature and in super-
natural calling, can be citizens of the one
people of God regardless of race or place or
time.[105] So the denial of moral absolutes on
the alleged basis of a radical change in concrete human nature cannot be sustained.

2. The "Preference" Principle and Moral Absolutes

Revisionists contend, as we have seen,
that the basic principle to guide us both in formulating "material" norms and in determin-
ing which human actions are permissible exceptions to them is the preference principle

or principle of proportionate good. According to this principle, moral judgments should be made by a comparative evaluation of the "nonmoral" goods and evils promised by the various alternatives; and the alternative promising the greater balance of nonmoral good over nonmoral evil is the one that ought to be chosen (i.e., the morally right action or sort of action). According to this principle it is morally right deliberately to intend a nonmoral evil for the sake of a proportionately "greater" nonmoral good. While some revisionists (e.g., Fuchs and Knauer) think that one does not, in any morally relevant sense, "intend" the evil when one chooses to do evil only as a proportionate means to a greater good, most revisionist theologians plainly acknowledge that the "preference" principle warrants the direct intending of evil that is done for the sake of a greater good. In fact, Schüller and McCormick, denying any morally relevant difference between an "intending" and a "permitting" will, consider it a commendable character trait to be willing deliberately to intend a lesser evil for the sake of a higher good, insofar as this bespeaks a greater love of the good. [106]

The "preference" principle has some plausibility. Indeed, to some revisionists it seems self-evidently true. According to the preference principle we are to choose the alternative promising the greater balance of good over evil. If this principle is not true, then the absurdity that we ought to choose the alternative promising the greater proportion of evil over good seems to follow. This, in fact, is the line of argument advanced by McCormick, who states the "preference" principle negatively to show how it is used in "conflict" situations in which evil inevitably results no matter what we choose to do. As McCormick puts it,

> The rule of Christian reason, if we are to be governed by the *ordo bonorum*, is to choose the lesser evil. This general statement, it would seem, is beyond debate, for the only alternative is that in conflict situations we should choose the greater evil, which is patently absurd. [107]

The plausibility of this principle, however, rests on the ambiguity of the word "good." The morally upright person naturally seeks to do the greater good, in the sense of what is morally good. But the revisionist "principle" assumes that it is possible to determine, prior

to choosing, which among various options is
morally good by balancing or measuring or
commensurating the various nonmoral goods
and evils in these different options. The problem here, as Germain Grisez, John Finnis,
and Joseph Boyle have shown, [108] is that there
simply is no unambiguous or homogeneous
measure according to which the goods in
question (goods such as human life itself,
health, knowledge of the truth, appreciation
of beauty, and friendship) can be compared
with one another or according to which individual instances of such goods (e.g., the life
of Mary Jones and the life of Peter Smith) can
be weighed or measured. Although none of
these goods is absolute – only God or the *Sum-
mum Bonum* is the absolute good – each is in
truth a priceless good of human persons and
as such a good to be prized, not priced, a good
participating in the incalculable goodness of
the human person. The attempt to weigh or
balance them against each other, to commensurate them, is like trying to compare the
number eighty-seven with the length of my
arm. One simply cannot do so. One could if
they could be reduced to some common denominator, as one can compare the number

eighty-seven with the length of my arm if one
compares these items by means of a common
denominator, such as centimeters, a scale
adopted not by discovering a truth but by an
arbitrary act of the will. The goods involved
in moral choices are not reducible to some
common denominator. They are simply different and incomparable goods of human
persons. Thus the presupposition upon which
the alleged "preference" principle is based is
false. One cannot determine, in a nonarbitrary way, which human goods are greater
and which are lesser. They are all incom-
parably good, irreducible aspects or dimen-
sions of human flourishing and well-being. [109]
And the same is true of the diverse instances
of the different goods of human persons.

Most revisionists, in fact, ignore this objection and simply continue to say that in
making moral judgments the goods and evils
at stake in the available alternatives are commensurable. The few who have tried to re-
spond to the objection have not succeeded.

McCormick, for example, has been forced
by this criticism to acknowledge that it is, in
the strict sense, impossible to commensurate
goods of different categories "against" each

other. Yet he now says that, "while the basic goods are not commensurable (one against the other), they are clearly associated" or interrelated. He then claims that one can, by considering these goods in their inter-relationship, judge that the deliberate choice to destroy an instance of one good in present circumstances will not undermine that good and that destroying or impeding it here and now is necessary in order to foster the flourishing of related goods.[110]

McCormick's response is inadequate. It amounts to saying that, although there is no nonarbitrary way to commensurate goods, we somehow succeed in doing so by "relating" or "associating" them. McCormick himself admits as much, for he speaks of assessing the greater good as a "prudent bet" and of commensurating in "fear and trembling" by *adopting* a hierarchy.[111] By saying this he is admitting that the commensuration required by the "preference" principle is accomplished by an act of choice. But the *principle* was advanced in order to determine, *prior* to choice, which possibilities are morally good and which are morally bad. Now McCormick says that to commensurate the goods in order to judge

which alternative promises the greater proportion of good over evil we must first adopt
a hierarchy and make prudent bets. This kind
of response simply will not do, nor does it face
squarely the criticism that the goods in question are simply not commensurable in the way
the "preference principle" requires them to
be.[112]

Garth Hallett claims that comparison of
goods is possible because the intelligibly appealing features of the various alternatives
can be said to have more or less "value," in
some sense of "value" that remains the same
as one moves from one feature to another. By
comparing goods in this way, he alleges, one
can discover the alternative promising the
greater good, for it will have *all* the "value"
promised by any other alternatives *and
more.*[113]

This reply, too, ends up in incoherence. As
John Finnis has noted, "If one option seems
to a deliberating agent to offer *all* that the
alternatives offer *and some more*, the alternatives simply fall away; they completely
lose the intelligible appeal which made them
options. . . .Morally significant choices. . .are
not and cannot be made in situations where

the alternatives to option X have *nothing* intelligibly attractive which X does not have, and X has *everything* the alternatives have, *and some.*"[114]

Two philosophers, Robert McKim and Peter Simpson (who are not, so far as I know, followers of revisionist thought) have argued that one who has identified, on the basis of the "preference principle," the option promising the greater proportion of good over evil can still choose an alternative excluded by the principle, perhaps out of selfishness.[115] This objection also misses the point of the criticism. The principle proposed by revisionists is not offered as a way for discerning the moral alternatives to selfishness or other immoral character traits. Nor is it the futile attempt to identify the morally right option *after* one has identified alternatives as selfish. Its purpose is to discover the morally right choice from among alternatives each of which has some intelligible appeal. And the insuperable difficulty it faces is that if it could succeed in doing so, the choice it was proposed to exclude as immoral would simply fade away, for only one alternative would be left that would be intelligibly appealing. It is possible for us to make immoral choices only because the intelligible goods promised by available options are *not* commensurable or reducible to some common denominator. Immoral choices are *unreasonable*, but not *irrational*.

Schüller and McCormick, as we have seen, in order to support the "preference principle" that requires us to do evil for the sake of a greater good, claim that a person who is willing to intend a lesser "nonmoral" evil for the sake of a greater "nonmoral" good has a greater willingness or love of the good – an admirable character trait – than one who refuses to do such evil. But this claim, as Finnis has noted, involves equivocal uses of the term "willing." Schüller and McCormick use it to designate emotional attitudes, not intelligent choices. But, as Finnis observes, "the moral life is in large measure a struggle to *integrate* one's feelings and attitudes, one's 'willingness and unwillingness,' with intelligent commitments. . .and choices."[116] On the Schüller-McCormick understanding of "willingness," it would seem to follow that a nation threatened by a ruthless adversary would have a greater love or will for the good if it is willing to execute the adversary's children in order to deter the adversary from carrying out planned injustices than if it is willing to defend itself by attacking the adversary but unwilling to hold its children hostage and execute them. Or a man willing to sign his name to a document setting forth beliefs that he does not hold in order to stay alive, care for his wife and children, and do noble deeds has a greater love of the good than, say, Thomas More, who was unwilling to do so. Such examples (and more could be added) show the fallacy of the Schüller-McCormick thesis, which equivocates in its use of the term "willing."

Another telling argument against the "preference principle" is advanced by Bartholomew Kiely, who observes that this principle fails to consider seriously the reflexive or immanent consequences of human acts as self-determining choices.[117] We make ourselves to be the persons we are by the actions we freely choose to do. In choosing to do evil, even for the sake of a "greater good," we make ourselves evildoers. I shall return to this point in the final part of this study.

The reasons set forth here (as well as

other objections to the "preference principle")[118] are sufficient to show that this alleged
principle must be rejected, and with it the
rationale it offers for denying moral absolutes.

3. The "Wholeness" or "Totality" of Human Acts and Moral Absolutes

As already noted, revisionists claim that
since we cannot determine whether a specific
act is morally good or bad without taking into account its "totality" or "wholeness," it
follows that there can be no moral absolutes.
According to revisionists such norms arbitrarily abstract the "material" or "physical"
character of the act from its human totality,
without any reference to the agent's purposes
or intentions.

Much that I said in the introduction to this
part is pertinent to this claim. For, as we have
seen, theologians who defend the truth of
moral absolutes do not ignore the purposes
or intentions of the agent; rather, they insist
that both the "remote" end and the "proximate" end of the agent's action, or both the
purpose for whose sake the deed is done and
the deed willingly chosen as a means to that
purpose, must be taken into account. It is, of

course, true that an act must be good in its "totality" or "wholeness" if it is to be morally good (*bonum ex integra causa*). But it is not true that we cannot judge that a proposed act is morally bad without taking into account *all* of its elements, for if we know that *any* of its elements is bad, the whole action is morally vitiated (*malum ex quocumque defectu*). Consequently, human acts already known to be bad by reason of their "objects" (i.e., the intelligible subject matter upon which the agent's will must bear as a chosen means to an end) remain morally bad even if the circumstances in which the person makes this choice or the end for whose sake it is made are good. Revisionists, in their arguments based on the "wholeness" or "totality" of the human act, focus on the agent's "remote" end or "further intention," that is, the good the agent hopes to realize by choosing to do X here and now. But they fail to take seriously the moral meaning of the X and the fact that the agent freely wills the X as a chosen means, the "proximate" end of his will act and the "present intention" that shapes his moral being. They are thus led to *redescribe* human actions in terms of their hoped-for results.

Thus they describe a series of intentionally contracepted marital acts not as acts of contraception but as an act of "fostering love responsibly toward a generous fecundity." Similarly, they describe the choice of contraceptive sterilization as a "marriage-stabilizing" act. But this is like describing the act of a mobster who plies his trade in order to support himself and his family as an act of "earning a living." It conceals, rather than reveals, *what* the person is doing.[119]

Thus the argument from the "wholeness" or "totality" of a human act to justify the denial of moral absolutes is fallacious.

4. The "Best" of the Catholic Tradition and Moral Absolutes

Revisionists, as we have seen, appeal to both St. Thomas and Vatican Council II to support their denial of moral absolutes. I shall first set forth the teaching of St. Thomas, which we have already seen in part, on the truth of moral absolutes, concluding my presentation of his thought with a comment on the text from the *Quaestiones Quodlibetales* to which Janssens and McCormick appeal as a "clincher" to their claim that Aquinas

was, like them, a proportionalist. I shall then
examine some relevant texts from Vatican
Council II.

That Aquinas affirms the truth of moral
absolutes can be seen from examining his
teaching on the precepts of the Decalogue. He
teaches that these precepts pertain to the
second *gradus* or set of natural law precepts,
as distinct from the first and third sets of such
precepts. To the first set belong such "common and first principles"[120] as "good is to be
done and pursued and evil is to be avoided,"[121]
"evil is to be done to no one,"[122] and "you are
to love your God and your neighbor."[123] To
the third set belong truths about human
action known only "by a more subtle consideration of reason." They are like conclusions drawn from the second set of natural
law precepts and are known only to the
"wise" – those in whom the virtue of prudence
is perfected and by whom those less virtuous
are to be instructed.[124]

Precepts comprising the second set of
natural law principles are known to be true
immediately by the natural reason of every-
one.[125] They are proximate conclusions from
the first indemonstrable principles of natural

law [126] and can be understood as true "immediately, with a little consideration" [127] even by
the most ordinary individual. [128] Such precepts
belong "absolutely" to the natural law. [129] But
since they can be obscured by sin and bad
habits, they have need for a further "edition,"
namely, through the divine [positive] law, [130]
and therefore they appear in the Decalogue.

Precepts of the Decalogue contain such
specific moral norms as those proscribing killing, adultery, and theft. Thomas regarded
these as absolutely binding – so much so that
not even God can dispense from them. [131] Properly to grasp his thought on this matter and
to understand his reply to such objections as
that Abraham, for instance, was morally
upright yet willing to kill his innocent son
Isaac, we need to distinguish, with Thomas,
between human acts described in their
"natural" species and human acts considered
in their "moral" species. According to
Aquinas, killing an innocent person, executing a convicted criminal, and killing an
assailant in an act of self-defense are all, in
their "natural" species, "acts of killing." [132] But
they differ in their "moral" species insofar as
only the killing of an innocent person is an

"act of killing" and as such morally bad *secundum se* [133] and contrary to the precept of the Decalogue, whereas the killings involved in executing a criminal and defending oneself by the measured use of force against unprovoked attack are partial aspects of morally good actions, specified morally by reason of the object of the will's choice *not* as acts of killing but as acts of justice and of legitimate self-defense. [134]

The basis for this distinction is that human acts, precisely as "human" or "moral," receive their "forms" not from nature but from human intelligence, which places them in their moral species by discerning their "ends," "objects," and "circumstances." Aquinas insists that all these factors must be good or in accord with natural law precepts if the whole human act is to be good. [135] He holds that the end and the object are the primary factors giving a human act its moral species. The end for whose sake an action is done is a primary source of an act's moral species because humans, as intelligent beings, act in the first place only for the sake of ends. [136] The end is the *forma magis universalis* of the whole human act in the same sense in which a genus

is said to be the *forma magis universalis* with
respect to its diverse species.[137] Nonetheless,
the "object" of the external act chosen and
commanded by the will is also a primary
source of the moral species of the whole
human act, precisely because this object is the
object of an act of will or of choice. Since it
is the "proximate" end that the acting person
intends,[138] it must be good if the whole human
act is to be good.

With these distinctions in mind, we find
St. Thomas's position on the precepts of the
Decalogue to be lucid. He holds that these
precepts are absolute, or exceptionless. They
are not mere formal norms or tautologies pro-
hibiting actions because they are "unjust," but
specific norms proscribing identifiable sorts
of human acts as absolutely immoral and contrary to the natural law. The moral objects
of the acts identified by these precepts are
specified descriptively as "killing the innocent," "coition with someone who is not one's
own [i.e., one's spouse]," and "taking what
belongs to another."[139] Aquinas teaches that
apparent exceptions to these norms are in
truth different kinds of human acts, specified
by different objects of human choice. Thus,

for Aquinas, the object of Abraham's act, when he was willing to obey God's command to sacrifice his son Isaac, was *not* the "killing of an innocent person" but the "carrying out of God's just command." God's command changed the situation, not by voluntaristically dissolving the obligation of the norm that we are not to kill the innocent, but by creating conditions in which the object and hence moral species of Abraham's chosen act was not killing the innocent but executing God's justice. [140]

Thus Aquinas affirms the truth of moral absolutes, namely, those natural law precepts proscribing acts specified as morally bad by reason of their "objects" (i.e., the intelligible subject matter upon which the will's act of choice bears). Among such absolutes are those proscribing killing of the innocent, adultery, theft, and fornication. [141] Thus, as we have already seen, when Thomas encounters the opinion of the "Old Scholiast" that adultery (sexual union with the tyrant's wife in this case) is morally permissible when done to save a nation from tyranny, he immediately replies, "the Commentator is not to be followed in this; one ought not commit adultery for the sake of any good whatsoever."[142]

Janssens and McCormick, as noted previously, appeal to a passage from St. Thomas's *Quaestiones Quodlibetales* to prove that he taught that it is morally right to intend a lesser premoral evil for the sake of a greater premoral good. They claim that in this passage he teaches that in some circumstances the premoral disvalue attached to some kinds of actions (e.g., killing), while remaining, is nonetheless justified by "outweighing circumstances."[143] But in the passage to which these authors refer, Aquinas expressly says that, when the circumstances make the act right – and circumstances can change the species of an act when they enter into the very "object" chosen[144] – the disorder or deformity of the act is *totally taken away.*[145] In other words, the act includes no "premoral evil" that is counterbalanced by some greater good. More significantly, in the very same text Aquinas says that there are some kinds of human acts that "have deformity inseparably annexed to them, such as fornication, adultery, and others of this sort, which can in no way be done morally."[146] Apparently, this passage in the text to which McCormick and Janssens

appeal to support their claim that Aquinas
was, like themselves, a proportionalist who
denied the truth of moral absolutes, escaped
their notice, for they do not mention it. Yet
it is a passage in which Aquinas affirms what
they deny: the truth of moral absolutes and
the intrinsic evil of certain sorts of human
acts as specified by their moral objects.

Similarly, appeals by revisionists to Vatican Council II to support their denial of moral
absolutes are notable because of their selec-
tivity. They refer to passages in which the
Council spoke of the complexity of *some* moral
problems, the fact that the gospel does not
give us the answers to *all* questions, and the
need to collaborate with others in discovering
the truth.[147] But they ignore passages impossible to reconcile with their denial of the truth
of moral absolutes. Thus, for instance, they
pass by in silence the text from *Gaudium et
Spes* in which the Council Fathers, after re-
affirming the "permanent binding force of
universal natural law and its all-embracing
precepts," teach that "actions which deliberately conflict with these same principles . . .
are criminal,"[148] and then declare that "*every*
act of war directed to the indiscriminate

destruction of whole cities or vast areas
with their inhabitants is a crime against God
and man, and merits unequivocal condemna-
tion."[149] They likewise ignore the teaching of
Gaudium et Spes that "*all* offenses against life
itself, such as murder, genocide, abortion,
euthanasia, and wilful self-destruction . . . are
criminal; they poison civilization, and they
debase their perpetrators more than their vic-
tims and militate against the honor of the
Creator."[150] Some of the actions absolutely
condemned in this passage are described in
terms which *can* be used in a morally
evaluative way (e.g., murder), and which
could thus be said to fall under the category
of the tautological "formal" norms recognized
as absolute by revisionists. But this, in fact,
is not the way the term "murder," for instance, has been used traditionally in docu-
ments of the magisterium. Thus, for example,
the *Catechismus Romanus* (popularly known
as the *Catechism of the Council of Trent*) quite
clearly indicated the kinds of killing properly
described by the term "murder."[151] Moreover,
other actions absolutely condemned in this
passage from *Gaudium et Spes* are definitely
described in terms recognized by revisionists

as morally neutral (e.g., abortion, euthanasia, wilful self-destruction). In short, Vatican Council II clearly affirmed the truth of moral absolutes and did not, as alleged by revisionists, support their denial.

For all the reasons given here, I think that the revisionist attack on the truth of moral absolutes has been shown to be based on seriously defective arguments. The failure of the revisionist effort to support the claim that there are no moral absolutes is itself evidence that there are moral absolutes. Now I will offer positive reasons to support the truth of such norms.

IV. The Truth of Moral Absolutes

I will begin my defense of the truth of moral absolutes by offering some reflections on the significance of human acts as free, self-determining choices. One of the criticisms advanced above against revisionist moral theology is that it fails to consider seriously the reflexive or immanent consequences of human acts as self-determining choices. Human acts, while involving physical performances, are not transient physical events in the material world that come and go; for at

their core is a free, self-determining choice
that abides within the person, giving to him
or her a character and a disposition to act in
the same way until a contradictory kind of
choice is made.[152] In short, we make ourselves
to be the kind of persons we are in and
through the actions we freely choose to do.

Here it is instructive to note that many
revisionist theologians maintain that the
terms "good" and "bad" refer most properly
to human persons as moral beings, whereas
the proper terms to use in referring to human
acts are "right" and "wrong." The "transcendent formal" norms that they recognize
as absolute are regarded by them, as we have
seen, as norms expressing the qualities, dispositions, and attitudes that ought to characterize the morally good person. These norms,
they say, are concerned *not* with human acts
but rather with the *being* of the human person as a moral being.[153] So-called "material"
norms, on the other hand, are not concerned
with the *being* of the person but with the
rightness or wrongness of human acts.[154]
Moreover, most revisionist theologians hold
a theory of "fundamental option" or "basic
freedom" that relocates self-determination

from the free choices we make every day
(including such basic commitments as getting
married or entering the priesthood or religious life) to an alleged exercise of a fundamental option or basic freedom at the core of
our being whereby, it is said, we take a stance
"for" or "against" God and basic human values.
In the exercise of this basic freedom we determine ourselves and make ourselves *to be* the
persons we are; according to these theologians, we do *not* basically determine ourselves
and make ourselves *to be* the persons we are
through the everyday exercise of free choice,
which, they maintain, is concerned with actions on the "periphery" of our existence.[155]
They even claim that a person *can* at times
freely choose to do what he or she believes
to be gravely immoral – for instance, to have
intercourse with the "wrong" person or to kill
an innocent human being without a proportionate reason – and still remain, in the core
of his or her being, a morally good person. In
short, for revisionists, the everyday deeds we
choose to do in exercising our "categorical"
freedom of choice "horizontally" in our daily
relationships are of a fundamentally different
moral character from the option we make

(apparently, in the thought of some revisionists, without even being consciously aware of
doing so)[156] deep within our being in our
"transcendental" relationship with God.

Revisionists maintain that our relationship
with God, established by the exercise of our
fundamental option, is directly related to our
salvation. They grant that our everyday,
"categorical" free choices are related to salvation, but only "indirectly," insofar as our many
acts of free choice must finally be integrated
into our fundamental option and bring it to
maturity.[157]

The Catholic tradition, however, affirms
the saving (or damning) significance of our
daily deeds – of the free choices we make
every day. Vatican Council II affirmed that
we will find perfected in heaven the very good
fruits of human nature and work that we nur-
ture here on earth.[158] The New Testament
teaches us that redemption includes all human
goods and the cosmos itself (see Rom 8.21;
1 Cor 3.22-23; Eph 1.10), and the Church pro-
claims that the spiritual and temporal orders,
while distinct, are so intimately linked in
God's plan that he intends in Christ to
appropriate the whole universe into a new

creation, "beginning here and now on earth and finding its fulfillment on the last day."[159]

The truth, in short, is that we determine our selves, our *being* as moral persons, in and through the actions we freely choose to do each day. When, for example, I choose to lie to my wife, perhaps about a minor matter and perhaps because I hope by doing so to preserve the "greater" good of family harmony, I make myself *to be* a liar; and I remain a liar, disposed to lie again, until, by another free choice, I become a repentant one. At the core of a human act is a free, self-determining choice.

In order that we become fully the beings God wills us to be, we must therefore make good moral choices. Choices are possible only where there are alternatives; our task is to discover, prior to choice, which alternatives are morally good and which are morally bad. Moral norms are thus "truths" intended to guide us in our choices.

But how are we to make true moral judgments and good moral choices? Here I suggest we follow the lead of St. Thomas (whose thought is so highly recommended to us by the magisterium), the teaching of

Vatican Council II, and the thought of many contemporary theologians, among them Germain Grisez and John Finnis. Following these sources we can see for ourselves the truth of moral absolutes.

St. Thomas included two kinds of "practical" truths among the first and common or indemonstrable *principles* of the natural law. The first kind included not only the proposition that the good is to be done and pursued and evil avoided, but also those propositions identifying the basic goods of human persons as forms of human flourishing that are to be pursued – such goods as life itself, handing on life to new generations and caring for that life, knowledge of the truth, and life in harmony and fellowship with others.[160] Although such "practical" truths govern our choices as human and intelligible, they do not serve to distinguish morally good alternatives of choice from those that are morally bad. But the second kind of "practical" truths included by St. Thomas among the first and common principles of natural law are truths that help us do this. Among these is the first principle that we are to love God and neighbor, the principle in light of which the truth of the precepts of the Decalogue can be seen. [161]

In other words, for St. Thomas the basic moral principle is not, as the revisionists would have it, "in freely choosing among alternatives, choose that alternative promising the greater proportion of nonmoral good over nonmoral evil," a principle that we have already found wanting. Rather, for him, the basic norm is that we should choose in such a way that we exhibit, in and through our choices, a true love of God and neighbor. This seems sound. Moreover, if we love God, we ought to accept from him his good gifts – the goods perfective of human persons. And if we love our neighbors, we ought to will that the goods of human existence flourish in them.

Vatican Council II likewise proposed a basic normative principle to direct human choices and actions. After noting that human action is important not only for its results but also and even more importantly because it develops human persons and gives to them, by reason of its self-determining and free character, their identity as moral beings, the Council declared:

Hence, the norm of human activity is this: that in accord with the divine plan and will, it should harmonize with the genuine good of the human race, and allow men as individuals and as members of society to pursue their total vocation and fulfill it. [162]

The fundamental principle of moral choice is further clarified, in my opinion, by the articulation given to it by Germain Grisez: "In voluntarily acting for human goods and avoiding what is opposed to them, one ought to choose and otherwise will those and only those possibilities whose willing is compatible with a will toward integral human fulfillment."[163] By this he means that in choosing among alternatives, we ought to choose those and only those alternatives whose willing is compatible with a love for all the goods of human persons and of the persons in whom these goods are meant to flourish.

A person about to choose in a morally wrong way does not respect and love the good gifts of God and the persons in whom these gifts are meant to exist. He or she chooses to act in a way that is not fully reponsive to the goods perfective of human persons.

From this it follows that we are not freely to choose to damage, destroy, or impede anything that is truly good either in ourselves or in others — whether out of hostility or because the continued flourishing of this good in ourselves or in others inhibits our participation in some other good that we arbitrarily prefer. [164] We ought not, then, freely choose to destroy the goods of innocent human life, exclusive marital friendship, justice, or other basic goods of human persons. Moral norms proscribing actions in which, of necessity, our will ratifies the deprivation of these goods are absolute, exceptionless.

Although moral absolutes are negative, they allow human persons to keep themselves open to be fully the beings they are meant to be. They remind us that some kinds of human choices and actions, although responsive to *some* aspects of human good, make us persons whose hearts are closed to the full range of human goods and to the persons in whom these goods are meant to flourish. Because the human person's vocation is to love, even as he or she has been and is loved by God in Christ, it is not possible to say, affirmatively, precisely what love requires, for its affirmative obligations must be discovered by us in our creative endeavor to grow daily in love of God and neighbor. Moral absolutes, however, show us what love *cannot* mean: it not mean that we set our wills *against* the good gifts that God wills to flourish in his children and close our hearts to our neighbors.

In and through the deeds we freely choose to do we give to ourselves our identities as moral beings. Moral absolutes remind us that by freely choosing to damage, destroy, or impede what is really good either in ourselves or in others – even for the noblest motives – we make ourselves to be evildoers. But human persons, made in the image of the holy and triune God, are to be, like him, absolutely innocent of evil. God wills properly and *per se* – that is, as end or means – only what is good. He permits evil, but does not choose to do evil.[165] Likewise, we, his children, ought never freely choose to do evil. Moral absolutes, therefore, are required by our *being* as moral beings, as persons capable of making ourselves to be the persons we are in and through the choices we freely make every day of our lives.

NOTES

1. For this see, for example, Pope John Paul II, Apostolic Exhortation, *Reconciliatio et Poenitentia*, n. 17; "Discourse to the International Congress of Moral Theology," 10 April 1986, n. 3, in *Persona, Verità e Morale: Atti del Congresso Internazionale di Teologia Morale (Roma, 7-12 aprile 1986)* (Rome: Città Nuova Editrice, 1987), p. 12.

2. See John R. Connery, S.J., *Abortion: The Development of the Roman Catholic Perspective* (Chicago: Loyola University Press, 1977) and Germain Grisez, *Abortion: The Myths, the Realities, and the Arguments* (New York: Corpus, 1970), pp. 137-50, 489-90. For what follows I am much in debt to Grisez's account.

3. *Didache*, 2.2: "ou phoneuseis, ou moicheuseis, ou paidophthoreseis, ou porneuseis. . .ou mageuseis, ou pharmakeuseis, ou phoneuseis teknon en phthora oude gennethen apokteineis. . . ." Greek text in Jean-Paul Audet, *La Didache: Instruction des Apotres* (Paris: Librairie Lecoffre, 1958), p. 228. English translation is that given in Grisez, *Abortion*, p. 138.

4. On this see John T. Noonan, Jr., "Abortion and the Catholic Church: A Summary History," *Natural Law Forum* 12 (1967): 90.

5. Clement of Alexandria, *Pedagogus*, 2.10:95-96: "Gamos de he paidopoiias orexis, ouch he tou spermatos ataktos ekkrisis. . .me kteinousi te to ek pronoias theikes phuomenon ton anthropon genos kakotechnois mechanais. Hautai gar porneias epikalummati tois es pantele katasposi phthoran phthoriois sugchromenai pharmakois examblis-

kousin hama to embruo ten philanthropian." Greek text in *Sources Chrétiennes*, no. 108, *Clement d'Alexandre, Le Pedagogue*, Livre II (Paris: Editions du Cerf, 1965), p. 184. Translation mine.

6. Tertullian, *Apologeticus*, 9.8: "Nobis vero, homicidio semel interdicto, etiam conceptum utero, dum adhuc sanguis in hominem delibatur dissolvere non licet. Homicidii festinatio est prohibere nasci; nec refert natam quis eripiat animam, an nascentem disturbet: homo est, et qui est futurus." Latin text in *Patrologiae Latinae Cursus Completus* (hereafter PL), ed. J. P. Migne, 1.319-20. Translation mine.

7. Basil the Great, *Epistle 138*: "phtheirasa kat epitedeusin, phonou diken hupechei. Akribologia de ekmemorphomenon kai anexeikonston par hemin ouk estin." Greek text in *Patrologiae Graecae Cursus Completus* (hereafter PG), ed. J. P. Migne, 36.672. Translation mine.

8. John Chrysostom, *Homilies on the Epistle to the Romans*, Homily 24: "mallon de kai phonou ti cheiron. . .ou gar techthenta anairei alla kai techthhenai koluei." Greek text in PG 60.626-27. Translation mine.

9. Ambrose, *Hexameron*, 5.18: ". . .quoque divites, ne per plures suum patrimonium dividatur, in utero proprios necant fetus et parricidalibus succis in ipso genitali alvo pignora sui ventris extinguunt, priusque aufertur vita, quam tradatur." Latin text in PL 14.231. Translation mine.

10. Ambrose, *Expositiones in Lucam*, 1.44: "Ille operatur et tu sacri uteri secretum incestas libidine? Vel pecudem imitare, vel Deum verere." Latin text in PL 15.1632. Translation mine.

11. Augustine, *De nuptiis et concupiscentia*, 1.15: "Produntur autem quando eo usque progrediuntur, ut exponant filios, qui nascentur invitis. Oderunt

enim nutrire vel habere quos gignere metuebant. Itaque cum in suos saevit, quos nolens genuit tenebrosa iniquitas, clara iniquitate in lucem promitur, et occulta turpitudo manifesta crudelitate convincitur. Aliquando eo usque pervenit haec libidinosa crudelitas, vel libido crudelis, ut etiam sterilitatis venena procuret; et si nihil valuerit, conceptus fetus aliquo modo intra viscera extinguat et fundat volendo suam prolem prius interire quam vivere, aut si in utero jam vivebat occidi antequam nasci." Latin text in PL 44.423-24. Translation by Peter Holmes and Robert Wallis in *A Library of Christian Fathers*, ed. P. Schaff, vol. 5, *St. Augustine* (New York: Christian Literature Co., 1887), p. 271.

12. It is worth noting that Augustine is not certain precisely when human life begins. Augustine, *Quaestiones in Heptateuchum*, 2.80; PL 34.626.

13. Augustine, *Contra Mendacium*, 7.18; PL 40.528-29.

14. Ibid.: "Quis ista nisi qui res humanae omnesque conatur mores legesque subvertere? Quod enim sceleratissimum facinus, quod turpissimum flagitium, quod impiissimum sacrilegium non dicatur posse fieri recte atque juste; nec impune tantum, verum etiam gloriose, ut in eo perpetrando, non solum supplicia nulla timeantur, sed sperantur et praemia, si semel concesserimus in omnibus malis operibus hominum ideo non quid fit, sed quare fiat esse quaerendum; ut quaecumque propter bonas causas facta inveniuntur, nec omnia mala esse judicentur?" Latin text in PL 40.529. English translation by Harold Jaffe in *Fathers of the Church*, vol. 16, *St. Augustine: Treatises on Various Subjects*, ed. Roy DeFerrari (New York: Fathers of the Church, 1952), p. 144.

15. Franz Scholz, "Problems on Norms Raised by Ethical Borderline Situations," in *Readings in Moral*

Theology No. 1: Moral Norms and the Catholic
Tradition, ed. Charles E. Curran and Richard A.
McCormick (New York: Paulist, 1979), pp. 158-83;
John Dedek, "Intrinsically Evil Acts: An Historical
Study of the Mind of St. Thomas," *Thomist* 43
(1979): 383-413; "Intrinsically Evil Acts: The
Emergence of a Doctrine," *Recherches de Théologie
Ancienne et Médiévale* 50 (1983): 191-226.

16. Dedek, "Intrinsically Evil Acts: The Emergence of
a Doctrine," 225-26.

17. See *Corpus Latinum Commentariorum in Aris-
totelem Graecorum*, 6.1, p. 239 (ad N.E. 1110a1-23):
"Christiana autem religio fatetur et tenet non esse
peccandum alicuius utilitatis consequendae vel alicuius incommodi vitandi gratia. Unde cum mentiri
et alienae uxori misceri utrumque sit peccare,
neutrum est aliquo modo faciendum." Translations
from Grosseteste, Albert, St. Thomas, Scotus, and
Suarez are my own.

18. Albert the Great, *Opera Omnia*, 14.1 (1968), pp.
124-25 (ad N.E. 1107a8-32), p. 380 (ad N.E.
1136b15-1137a30) "Commentator falsum dicit."

19. Thomas Aquinas, *De Malo,* q. 15, a. 1, 5: "Illud quod
est peccatum ex genere, non licet fieri quocumque
bono fine, secundum illud Rom. 3,8 . . . . Sed sicut
dicit Commentator 5 Ethic., epices, id est vir vir-
tuosus, committit adulterium cum uxore tyranni, ut
tyrannum interficiens liberet patriam. Ergo et
adulterium non est secundum se peccatum. Multo
ergo minus alius fornicationis actus."

20. Ibid., ad 5: "Ille Commentator in hoc non est
sustinendus: pro nulla enim utilitate debet aliquis
adulterium committere."

21. Duns Scotus, *Ordinatio Scoti*, I, d. 44, q. 1: "omnes
qui subsunt legi divinae, si non agunt secundum
illam, inordinate agunt."

22. Ibid., III, d. 37, q. un., ad 3: "tenebantur omnes ad ista praecepta, quae erant praecepta interius in corde cuiuslibet, vel forte per aliquam doctrinam exteriorem datam a patribus ad filios, licet non essent tunc scripta in libro."

23. Ibid., III, d. 37, q. un.

24. Ibid.: "necessario sequentes ex eis. . .strictissime dicuntur de lege naturae. . .et in talibus non potest esse dispensatio."

25. Ibid.: "Est amandus ut Deus solus."

26. Ibid., IV, d. 46, q. 1, n. 3.

27. Ibid., IV, d. 28, q. un., n. 6: "nullus. . .actus est bonus in genere ex solo obiecto, nisi amare Deum. . .et solus actus est ex genere malus, qui est oppositus isto actui, respectu eiusdem obiecti, ut odisse Deum, qui nullo modo potest circumstantionari, ut sit bonus. . .omnis alius actus est indifferens, qui est respectu alterius obiecti, et potest circumstantion- abilis bene aut male."

28. On *potentia absoluta* and *potentia ordinata* see ibid., I, d. 44. On dispensations from the Decalogue, see ibid., III, d. 37, q. un.

29. Francis Suarez, *De legibus ac de Deo Legislatore*, II, 5, n. 14.

30. Ibid., II, 6, n. 8: "Deus, ut auctor talis naturae, praecipit id facere vel vitare quod ratio dicit esse faciendum vel vitandum. . .quidquid contra rationem rectam fit, displicet Deo et contrarium illi placet, quia cum voluntas Dei sit summa iusta, non potest illi non displicere quod turpe est, nec non placere honestum."

31. Ibid., II, 6, n. 17: "in actu humano esse aliquam bonitatem vel malitiam ex vi obiecti praecise spec- tati, ut est consonum vel dissonum rationi rectae et secundum eam posse denominari."

32. Ibid., II, 6, n. 23: "Deus non potest non prohibere ea quae sunt intrinsice mala per aliquam legem. . . supposita voluntate creandi naturam rationalem cum sufficienti cognitione ad operandum non potuisse Deum non velle prohibere tali creaturae actus intrinsice malos vel nolle praecipere honestos necessarios."

33. Ibid., II, 15, nn. 7, 8, 18, 19, 25, 30.

34. John C. Ford, S.J., and Germain Grisez, "Contraception and the Infallibility of the Ordinary Magisterium," *Theological Studies* 39 (1978): 258-312, at 279-80.

35. John T. Noonan, Jr., *Contraception: A History of Its Treatment by Catholic Theologians and Canonists* (Cambridge: Harvard University Press, Belknap Press, 1965).

36. In a document included in the "majority report," the *Documentum Syntheticum de Moralitate Nativitatum*, the majority explicitly repudiated as absolutely immoral anal and oral sex. See text in *The Birth-Control Debate*, ed. Robert Hoyt (Kansas City, MO: The National Catholic Reporter, 1969), p. 76.

37. Charles E. Curran, "Divorce from the Perspective of Moral Theology," in *Proceedings of the Canon Law Society of America 1974* (Washington, DC: Canon Law Society of America, 1974), p. 6.

38. *Documentum Syntheticum*, in Hoyt, p. 69.

39. By "conjugal acts which by intention are infertile" the authors of the *Documentum Syntheticum* mean marital acts chosen during the wife's infertile period. The authors see no moral difference between the use of "artificial" contraceptives and abstinence from intercourse during the wife's fertile time.

40. *Documentum Syntheticum*, in Hoyt, p. 72.

41. Ibid., p. 75.

42. On this see the *Schema Documenti de Responsabili Paternitate*, another document included in the "majority report," in Hoyt, pp. 88-90.

43. Josef Fuchs, "Naturrecht oder naturalistischer Fehlschluss?" *Stimmen der Zeit* 29 (1988): 409, 420-22; Fuchs, *Christian Ethics in a Secular Arena* (Washington, DC: Georgetown University Press, 1984), p. 75; Fuchs, *Personal Responsibility and Christian Morality* (Washington, DC: Georgetown University Press, 1983), pp. 131, 139.

44. Louis Janssens, "Ontic Evil and Moral Evil," *Louvain Studies* 4 (1972): 144 (reprinted in *Readings in Moral Theology No. 1*, pp. 72-73); "Norms and Priorities in a Love Ethic," *Louvain Studies* 6 (1977): 231.

45. E.g., Timothy O'Connell, *Principles for Catholic Morality* (New York: Seabury, 1978), pp. 157-58.

46. Janssens, "Norms and Priorities in a Love Ethic," 207; O'Connell, *Principles*, pp. 158-59.

47. In addition to the authors cited in note 46 see Richard Gula, *What Are They Saying About Moral Norms?* (New York: Paulist, 1982), pp. 55-56.

48. Fuchs, *Christian Ethics in a Secular Arena*, p. 72.

49. Janssens, "Norms and Priorities in a Love Ethic," 208.

50. Fuchs, *Christian Ethics in a Secular Arena*, p. 72; see Fuchs, "Naturrecht oder naturalistischer Fehlschluss?" 411, 416, 419; see also Richard McCormick, *Notes on Moral Theology 1965-1980* (Lanham, MD: University Press of America, 1981), pp. 578-79.

51. Dedek, "Intrinsically Evil Acts: The Emergence of a Doctrine," 191; Fuchs, *Personal Responsibility and Christian Morality*, p. 191; Fuchs, *Christian Ethics in a Secular Arena*, p. 74; Janssens, "Norms and Priorities in a Love Ethic," 210, 216.

52. Francis Sullivan, *Magisterium: Teaching Authority in the Catholic Church* (New York: Paulist Press, 1983), pp. 150-51. Sullivan lists Curran, Böckle, Fuchs, Schüller, Häring, and other revisionists as agreeing with this way of presenting the matter.

53. Fuchs, *Personal Responsibility and Christian Morality*, p. 129.

54. Ibid., p. 133.

55. Ibid., p. 124.

56. Sullivan, *Magisterium*, pp. 151-52; see Fuchs, *Personal Responsibility and Christian Morality*, p. 140.

57. Fuchs, *Personal Responsibility and Christian Morality*, p. 142.

58. See Daniel Maguire, *Death by Choice* (New York: Doubleday, 1974), p. 99; Janssens, "Norms and Priorities in a Love Ethic," 217.

59. O'Connell, *Principles for Catholic Morality*, p. 162.

60. Fuchs, *Personal Responsibility and Christian Morality*, pp. 140-42; Janssens, "Norms and Priorities in a Love Ethic," 217-18.

61. "Premoral" is the term used by Fuchs; "nonmoral" is preferred by Schüller, McCormick, and others; "ontic" is used by Janssens and others.

62. See above, note 38.

63. Schüller, "What Ethical Principles Are Universally Valid?" *Theology Digest* 19 (March 1971): 24 (translation of "Zur Problematik allgemeinen ethischer Grundsätze," *Theologie und Philosophie* 45 [1970]: 4). McCormick's comment on this text is of interest. He writes: "Stated negatively, it [this principle] reads: put in a position where he will unavoidably cause evil, man must discover which is the worst evil and avoid it. Stated positively, this is its formulation: put before two concurring but mutually exclusive values, man should discover

which must be preferred and act accordingly. These statements imply that a physical evil can be caused or permitted only if it is demanded by a proportionate good" (*Notes on Moral Theology 1965-1980*, p. 315).

64. McCormick, "Ambiguity in Moral Choice," The Père Marquette Lecture, 1973, as reprinted in *Doing Evil to Achieve Good*, ed. Richard McCormick and Paul Ramsey (Chicago: Loyola University Press, 1978), p. 39.

65. Fuchs, *Personal Responsibility and Christian Morality*, p. 138.

66. For justification of directly intended abortion for a "commensurate" or "proportionate" reason see Charles E. Curran, *New Perspectives in Moral Theology* (Notre Dame: University of Notre Dame Press, 1974), pp. 190-91. For mercy killing or euthanasia, see Maguire, *Death by Choice*.

67. Peter Knauer, "The Hermeneutic Function of the Principle of Double Effect," in *Readings in Moral Theology No. 1*, pp. 10-11.

68. Fuchs, *Personal Responsibility and Christian Morality*, p. 136.

69. McCormick, "Ambiguity in Moral Choice," as reprinted in *Doing Evil to Achieve Good*, pp. 30-31; see also pp. 35-36.

70. Bruno Schüller, "The Double Effect in Catholic Thought: A Revolution," in *Doing Evil to Acheive Good*, p. 191. See McCormick, "A Commentary on the Commentaries," ibid., p. 241.

71. As cited by McCormick, "A Commentary on the Commentaries," pp. 241, 243.

72. Schüller, "The Double Effect in Catholic Thought," p. 191, emphasis in the original.

73. McCormick, "A Commentary on the Commentaries," p. 241.

74. See above, note 40.
75. Fuchs, *Personal Responsibility and Christian Morality*, p. 138.
76. See authors cited above in note 51.
77. Janssens, "Ontic Evil and Moral Evil," 144; Janssens, "Norms and Priorities in a Love Ethic," 231.
78. Fuchs, *Christian Ethics in a Secular Arena*, p. 82; Fuchs, *Personal Responsibility and Christian Morality*, pp. 142, 212; K.H. Peschke, "Tragfähigkeit und Grenzen des Prinzips der Doppelwirkung," *Studia Moralia* 26 (1988): 107; Franz Böckle, *Fundamental Moral Theology* (New York: Pueblo, 1980), pp. 236-37.
79. McCormick, "A Commentary on the Commentaries," p. 241.
80. See note 16 above.
81. Scholz, "Problems on Norms Raised by Ethical Borderline Situations," pp. 163-65; McCormick, *Notes on Moral Theology 1965-1980*, pp. 582-84, 767 n. 52.
82. Constant appeal is made by the revisionists to the passage in *Summa Theologiae*, 1-2, 94, 4, where St. Thomas speaks of norms that "valent ut in pluribus," but are subject to exceptions "ut in paucioribus."
83. Janssens, "Ontic Evil and Moral Evil," 125-26.
84. Ibid., 133, 139-41.
85. John Milhaven, "Moral Absolutes in Thomas Aquinas," in *Absolutes in Moral Theology?* ed. Charles E. Curran (Washington, D.C.: Corpus Books, 1968), pp. 150-51; Dedek, "Intrinsically Evil Acts: An Historical Study of the Mind of St. Thomas," 408-09.
86. The text in question is found in *Quaestiones Quodlibetales*, 9, q. 7, a. 2.

MORAL ABSOLUTES   87

87. Janssens, "Norms and Priorities in a Love Ethic,"
    232; McCormick, "Moral Theology Since Vatican II:
    Clarity or Chaos?" *Cross Currents* 29 (Spring 1979):
    21.

88. Thus Sullivan, *Magisterium*, p. 155, appeals to texts
    from *Gaudium et Spes*, nn. 16, 33, and 46 to sup-
    port the revisionist position.

89. Dedek, "Intrinsically Evil Acts: The Emergence of
    a Doctrine," 191; Fuchs, *Christian Ethics in a
    Secular Arena*, p. 74; Janssens, "Norms and
    Priorities in a Love Ethic," 210, 216.

90. Pope John Paul II, *Reconciliatio et Poenitentia*, n.
    17, says that these acts are always seriously wrong
    "per se ipsos et in se ipsis, extra adiuncta, propter
    objectum suum."

91. Thomas Aquinas, *In II Sent.*, d. 40, q. un., a. 1, ad
    4; *In IV Sent.*, d. 16, q. 3, a. 1b, ad 2; *Summa
    Theologiae*, 1-2, 1, 3, ad 3; *De Malo*, q. 2, a. 4c. See
    Karl Hoermann, "Das Objekt als Quelle der Sitt-
    lichkeit," in *The Ethics of St. Thomas Aquinas*, ed.
    L. Elders (Vatican City: Libreria Editrice Vaticana,
    1984), pp. 122-23, 126-28; Martin Rhonheimer,
    Natur als Grundlage der Moral (Innsbruck and
    Vienna: Tyrolia Verlag, 1987), p. 95; and Theo
    Belmans, *Le sens objectif de l'agir humain* (Vatican
    City: Libreria Editrice Vaticana, 1980), pp. 214-16.

92. Thomas Aquinas, *Summa Theologiae*, 1-2, 20, 2; *In
    II Sent.*, d. 40, q. un., a. 2.

93. For texts from St. Thomas, analysis, and commen-
    tary see Patrick Lee, "The Permanence of the Ten
    Commandments: St. Thomas and His Modern Com-
    mentators," *Theological Studies* 42 (1981): 431-32;
    Belmans, *Le sens objectif de l'agir humain*, pp. 62,
    109-19, 124, 162, 237; Rhonheimer, *Der Natur als
    Grundlage der Moral*, pp. 91-99, 317-45, 367-74.

94. Thus "direct" killing of the innocent is always ex-
plained as killing intended by the will either as an
end or as a means. See Pope Pius XII, *Discorsi e
Radiomessagi di sua Santità Pio XII* 6 (12
November 1949), 191-92; Pope Paul VI, *Humanae
Vitae*, note 14; Congregation for the Doctrine of the
Faith, *De Abortu Procurato* (18 November 1974), n.
7, and *Donum Vitae* (22 February 1987), note 20.

95. Thomas Aquinas, *In II Sent.*, d. 40, q. 1, a. 1, ad 4;
Summa Theologiae, 1-2, 1, 3, ad 3.

96. Sullivan, *Magisterium*, pp. 151-52.

97. On this see Germain Grisez, "Moral Absolutes: A
Critique of the View of Josef Fuchs, S.J.," *Anthro-
pos: Rivista di Studi sulla Persona e la Famiglia*
1 (1985): 170. This journal is now called *Anthropotes*.

98. Fuchs, *Personal Responsibility and Christian
Morality*, p. 129.

99. Grisez, "Moral Absolutes," 172.

100. Fuchs, "Naturrecht oder naturalistischer Fehl-
schluss?" 409, 420-22; Fuchs, *Christian Ethics in a
Secular Arena*, p. 75; McCormick, *Notes on Moral
Theology 1965-1980*, pp. 710-11.

101. Janssens, "Ontic Evil and Moral Evil," 144; "Norms
and Priorities in a Love Ethic," 231.

102. Sullivan, *Magisterium*, p. 152; Karl Rahner, "Basic
Observations on the Subject of the Changeable and
Unchangeable Factors in the Church," *Theological
Investigations*, vol. 14 (New York: Herder & Herder,
1976), pp. 14-15.

103. *Gaudium et Spes*, n. 29; *Lumen Gentium*, n. 19.

104. *Lumen Gentium*, n. 13.

105. *Gaudium et Spes*, n. 29; *Lumen Gentium*, n. 13.

106. See above, notes 69 to 73.

107. McCormick, "Ambiguity in Moral Choice," as
reprinted in *Doing Evil to Achieve Good*, p. 38.

108. Germain Grisez, "Against Consequentialism," *American Journal of Jurisprudence* 23 (1978): 21-72; Grisez, *The Way of the Lord Jesus*, vol. 1, *Christian Moral Principles* (Chicago: Franciscan Herald Press, 1983), pp. 141-72; John Finnis, *Natural Law and Natural Rights* (Oxford: Oxford University Press, The Clarendon Press, 1980), pp. 118-25; Finnis, *Fundamentals of Ethics* (Washington, DC: Georgetown University Press, 1983), pp. 86-105; John Finnis, Joseph M. Boyle, Jr., and Germain Grisez, *Nuclear Deterrence, Morality, and Realism* (New York: Oxford University Press, 1987), pp. 254-61.

109. In *Nuclear Deterrence, Morality, and Realism* Finnis, Boyle, and Grisez show how the revisionist principle is incompatible with free choice. They note that this principle requires that "two conditions be met: (i) that a morally significant choice be made and (ii) that the person making it be able to identify one option as offering unqualifiedly greater good or lesser evil. But these two conditions are incompatible, and in requiring that they be met simultaneously consequentialism is incoherent" (p. 254). As they show, choice is possible only when there are two or more alternatives. But an alternative exists only when the good it promises is not available in other possibilities. Thus if condition (ii) is met, condition (i) cannot be, and vice versa.

110. McCormick, "A Commentary on the Commentaries," in *Doing Evil to Achieve Good*, p. 227; see also pp. 251-53.

111. Ibid.

112. McCormick's response has been criticized by Finnis in *Fundamentals of Ethics*, pp. 99-105, and by Grisez in *Christian Moral Principles*, pp. 161-64.

113. Garth Hallett, "The 'Incommensurability' of Values," *Heythrop Journal* 28 (1987): 373-87.

114. Finnis, *Moral Absolutes: Tradition, Revision, and Truth*, The Michael J. McGivney Lectures for 1988, forthcoming. Professor Finnis kindly sent me a copy of the draft of this work, in which his criticism of Hallett is given.

115. Robert McKim and Peter Simpson, "On the Alleged Incoherence of Consequentialism," *New Scholasticism* 62 (1988): 349-52.

116. Finnis, "The Act of the Person," in *Persona, Verità e Morale*, p. 172.

117. Bartholomew Kiely, "The Impracticality of Proportionalism," *Gregorianum* 66 (1985): 656-66.

118. In addition to the works by Grisez, Finnis, Kiely, Rhonheimer, Belmans, Lee, and Hoermann already cited in previous notes, see Servais Pinckaers, *Ce qu'on ne peut jamais faire: La question des actes intrinséquement mauvais. Histoire et discussion* (Freiburg: Editions Universitaires; Paris: Editions du Cerf, 1986); John R. Connery, "Catholic Ethics: Has the Norm for Rule-Making Changed?" *Theological Studies* 42 (1981): 232-50; William E. May, "Aquinas and Janssens on the Moral Meaning of Human Acts," *Thomist* 48 (1984): 566-606.

119. On this, see the text cited in notes 91-95 above. Also see Eric D'Arcy, *Human Acts: An Essay on Their Moral Evaluation* (New York: Oxford University Press, 1963), pp. 18-25.

120. Thomas Aquinas, *Summa Theologiae*, 1-2, 100, 1.

121. Ibid., 1-2, 94, 2.

122. Ibid., 1-2, 95, 2.

123. Ibid., 1-2, 100, 3, ad 1.

124. Ibid., 1-2, 100, 1.

125. Ibid.

126. Ibid., 1-2, 100, 3.

127. Ibid., 1-2, 100, 1.

128. Ibid., 1-2, 100, 11.

129. Ibid., 1-2, 100, 1.

130. Ibid., 1-2, 100, 11.

131. Ibid., 1-2, 100, 8.

132. Ibid., 1-2, 1, 3, ad 3; see *In II Sent.*, d. 40, q. 1, a. 2, ad 4.

133. *Summa Theologiae*, 2-2, 64, 6.

134. Ibid., 2-2, 64, 2, on execution of criminals as an act of justice; and 64, 7, on self-defense.

135. Ibid., 1-2, 18, entire question.

136. Ibid., 1-2, 18, 1-3.

137. Ibid., 1-2, 1, 7c and ad 3.

138. Ibid., 1-2, 20, 2.

139. Ibid., 1-2, 100, 8.

140. See Lee, "Permanence of the Ten Commandments," for a detailed examination of relevant texts from St. Thomas.

141. On killing the innocent, see *Summa Theologiae*, 2-2, 64, 6; on adultery, 2-2, 154, 8; on theft, 2-2, 64, 5 and 6; on fornication, 2-2, 154, 2.

142. *De Malo*, q. 15, a. 1, ad 15.

143. Janssens, "Norms and Priorities in a Love Ethic," 232; McCormick, "Moral Theology since Vatican II: Clarity or Chaos?" 21.

144. On this see *Summa Theologiae*, 1-2, 18, 10.

145. Thomas Aquinas, *Quaestiones Quodlibetales*, 9, q. 7, a. 2: "aliae circumstantiae possunt supervenire ita honestantes actum, quod *praedictae inordinationes totaliter evacuuntur.*"

146. Ibid.: "Quaedam enim sunt quae habent deformitatem inseparabiliter annexam, ut fornicatio, adulterium, et alia huiusmodi, *quae nullo modo bene fieri possunt.*"

147. Appeal is made to *Gaudium et Spes*, nn. 16, 33, 46. See note 88 above.

148. *Gaudium et Spes*, n. 79.

149. Ibid., n. 80.

150. Ibid., n. 27.

151. *Catechismus ex decreto Ss. Concilii Tridentini ad Parochos, Pii V., Pont. Max., iussu editus* (Rome: Propagandae Fidei, 1869) 2:123-31 (on the fifth commandment). The treatment of "murder" carefully sets out cases which are not murder: (1) killing animals; (2) capital punishment; (3) killing in just war; (4) killing in obedience to a divine command; (5) accidental killing; and (6) killing in self-defense. Once these cases have been set aside, the absoluteness of the commandment is asserted very lucidly: "These, which we have just mentioned, are the cases not contemplated by the commandment; and with these exceptions, the prohibition embraces all others, with regard to the person who kills, the person killed, and the means used to kill. As to the person who kills, the commandment recognizes no exception whatever. . . .With regard to the person killed, the obligation of the law is no less extensive, embracing every human creature. . . .Finally, if we consider the numerous means by which murder may be committed, the law makes no exception." This catechism has special status since it was launched by the Council of Trent, published with the authority of many popes (first edition, 1566), translated into many languages, and used for centuries all over the world.

152. On this see Grisez, *Christian Moral Principles*, pp. 41-59.

153. See above, note 47.

154. Janssens, "Norms and Priorities," 209.

155. On fundamental option and the radical difference between ordinary free choices and fundamental option in the mind of revisionists see, for instance, Fuchs, *Human Values and Christian Morality* (Dublin: Gill and Macmillan, 1970), pp. 92-112, esp. 96-98.

156. A good critique of the revisionist understanding of fundamental option is given by Joseph M. Boyle, Jr., "Freedom, the Human Person, and Human Acts," in *Principles of Christian Moral Life*, ed. William E. May (Chicago: Franciscan Herald Press, 1980), pp. 237-66.

157. Fuchs, *Human Values and Christian Morality*, p. 96.

158. *Gaudium et Spes*, n. 39.

159. *Apostolicam Actuositatem*, n. 5.

160. *Summa Theologiae*, 1-2, 94, 2.

161. Ibid., 1-2, 100, 8, ad 3.

162. *Gaudium et Spes*, n. 35.

163. Grisez, *Christian Moral Principles*, p. 184.

164. Here I have briefly summarized the thrust of the seventh and eighth "modes of responsibility" set forth by Grisez, ibid., pp. 215-16. On the "modes of responsibility" see ibid., pp. 205-25.

165. That God is totally innocent of evil and only permits it is taught by the Council of Trent, Session VI, in *Enchiridion Symbolorum*, ed. Henricus Denzinger and Albertus Schonmetzer, 33rd ed. (Rome: Herder, 1983), n. 1556. For pertinent texts from St. Thomas and discussion see Lee, "Permanence of the Ten Commandments," 455-56.

The Père Marquette Lectures in Theology

1969: "The Authority for Authority,"
by Quentin Quesnell
Professor of Theology
Marquette University

1970: "Mystery and Truth,"
by John Macquarrie
Professor of Theology
Union Theological Seminary, New York

1971: "Doctrinal Pluralism,"
by Bernard Lonergan, S.J.
Professor of Theology
Regis College, Ontario

1972: "Infallibility,"
by George A. Lindbeck
Professor of Theology
Yale University

1973: "Ambiguity in Moral Choice,"
by Richard A. McCormick, S.J.
Professor of Moral Theology
Bellarmine School of Theology

1974: "Church Membership as a Catholic
and Ecumenical Problem,"
by Avery Dulles, S.J.
Professor of Theology
Woodstock College

1975: "The Contributions of Theology to
Medical Ethics,"
by James Gustafson
University Professor of Theological Ethics
University of Chicago

1976: "Religious Values in an Age of Violence,"
by Rabbi Marc Tannenbaum
Director of National Interreligious Affairs
American Jewish Committee, New York City

1977: "Truth Beyond Relativism: Karl Mannheim's
Sociology of Knowledge,"
by Gregory Baum
Professor of Theology and Religious Studies
St. Michael's College

1978: "A Theology of 'Uncreated Energies' "
by George A. Maloney, S.J.
Professor of Theology
John XXIII Center For Eastern Christian
Studies
Fordham University

1980: "Method in Theology: An Organon For Our
Time,"
by Frederick E. Crowe, S.J.
Research Professor in Theology
Regis College, Toronto

1981: "Catholics in the Promised Land of the Saints,"
by James Hennesey, S.J.
Professor of the History of Christianity
Boston College

1982: "Whose Experience Counts in
Theological Reflection?"
by Monika Hellwig
Professor of Theology
Georgetown University

1983: "The Theology and Setting of Discipleship in
the Gospel of Mark,"
by John R. Donahue, S.J.
Professor of Theology
Jesuit School of Theology, Berkeley

1984: "Should War be Eliminated?
Philosophical and Theological Investigations,"
by Stanley Hauerwas
Professor of Theology
Notre Dame University

1985   "From Vision to Legislation:
        From the Council to a Code of Laws,"
        by Ladislas M. Orsy, S.J.
        Professor of Canon Law
        Catholic University of America
        Washington, D.C.

1986   "Revelation and Violence:
        A Study in Contextualization,"
        by Walter Brueggemann
        Professor of Old Testament
        Eden Theological Seminary
        St. Louis, Missouri

1987   "Nova Et Vetera: The Theology of Tradition
        in American Catholicism,"
        by Gerald Fogarty
        Professor of Religious Studies
        University of Virginia

1988   "The Christian Understanding of Freedom and
        the History of Freedom in the Modern Era:
        The Meeting and Confrontation Between
        Christianity and the Modern Era in a
        Postmodern Situation,"
        by Walter Kasper
        Professor of Dogmatic Theology
        University of Tübingen

1989   "Moral Absolutes: Catholic Tradition, Current
        Trends, and the Truth,"
        by William E. May
        Ordinary Professor of Moral Theology
        The Catholic University of America

Uniform format, cover and binding.

Copies of this Lecture and the others in the
series are obtainable from:

        Marquette University Press
        Marquette University
        Milwaukee, Wisconsin 53233, U.S.A.